TELL MY PRIESTS

Words of Our Lord to Priests about His Mercy
As Revealed to St. Maria Faustina Kowalska

Compiled by
Father George W. Kosicki, C.S.B.

MARIAN PRESS
STOCKBRIDGE, MA 01263

2007

Available from:

Association of Marian Helpers, Stockbridge, MA 01263

Prayerline:	1-800-804-3823
Orderline:	1-800-462-7426
Website:	www.marian.org

Cover Design: Catherine M. LeVesque

Library of Congress Catalog Card Number 87-62982
ISBN 978-0-944203-08-8

TABLE OF CONTENTS

PRAYER for PRIESTS

*O my Jesus, I beg You on behalf of the whole Church:
Grant it love and the light of Your Spirit, and **give power to the
words of priests** so that hardened hearts might be brought to
repentance and return to You, O Lord. Lord, **give us holy
priests;** You yourself maintain them in holiness. O Divine and
Great High Priest, may the power of Your mercy accompany
them everywhere and **protect them from the devil's traps and
snares which are continually being set for the souls of priests.**
May the power of Your mercy, O Lord, shatter and bring to
naught all that might tarnish the sanctity of priests, for You
can do all things.*

Prayer of Sister Faustina from Diary (1052)

PREFACE

Father Daniel Callarn, C.S.B., a fellow Basilian and editor of the Canadian Catholic Review, wrote an article on Sister Faustina from materials sent to him from the Marian Helpers in Stockbridge, Mass., which appeared in the July/August 1985 issue. It so well captured the life and role of Sr. Faustina as an apostle of God's Mercy that the adapted article is presented here as the preface.

SISTER FAUSTINA H. KOWALSKA (1905-1938)

Private revelations have been important to the Church from the time of the apostles (cf 2 Cor 12) to the present. No age has been without its visionaries: Ambrose, Gregory the Great, Francis of Assisi, Joan of Arc, Teresa of Avila…; and the Marian shrines, such as Lourdes and Fatima, witness to the continuation of the phenomenon. One of the most popular Catholic devotions — to the Sacred Heart of Jesus — was greatly stimulated by the revelations made to St. Margaret Mary Alacoque between 1673 and 1675. In the twentieth century a similar devotion has been of particular importance to the people of Poland, especially during the harsh ordeal of the Second World War and its aftermath. Throughout the country an image of Christ with rays of red and clear light streaming from his breast was displayed, bringing courage and perseverance to millions of people. The caption under the image was "Jesus, I Trust in You," and the new devotion was dedicated to The Divine Mercy.

One Pole strengthened by this devotion was Karol Wojtyla. At the sanctuary of Merciful Love (Collevalenza, Italy) in 1964 he described The Divine Mercy as:

> The mercy which provides the dignity of the human person everywhere. We often think of it is Poland from where I have come for the Council with the other Polish Bishops… we think of the mercy of Christ, of the mercy of God.

As Pope John Paul II, he drew upon the devotion in writing his encyclical *Dives in Misericordia* (Rich in Mercy). In 1981, again at Collevalenza, he reiterated his commitment to the message of divine mercy:

> Right from the beginning of my ministry in St. Peter's See in Rome I considered this message my special task. Providence has assigned it to me in the present situation of man, the Church, and the world....

The origins of the devotion in its contemporary form lie in the revelations made during the 1930s to a young nun, Sister Faustina (Helena Kowalska), who had been born near Lodz (central Poland in 1905, the third of ten children. In this case, the hagiographical cliches were true: her parents were poor but pious, and she exhibited signs of holiness. At the age of twenty she joined the Sisters of Our Lady of Mercy, a community dedicated to helping young women in distress. This was her work until her death from tuberculosis thirteen years later, in 1938. She was canonized by Pope John Paul II in 2000 as the first saint of the Great Jubilee Year. At her canonization, John Paul II also established the Feast of Divine Mercy for the entire Church.

Sister Faustina's convent duties were ordinary — serving in the kitchen, the bakery, the garden, answering the door — but in this humble setting she underwent remarkable and extensive mystical experiences. In obedience to her spiritual director, she began to record these experiences in 1934. Her notebooks, termed the "*Diary*" amount to 600 printed pages. In her visions, Jesus told her to record all of the statements about His mercy because they would encourage souls not to be fearful when they approached Him. The *Diary* also unveils the interior life of Sister Faustina to reveal a person demanding of herself whether undergoing illuminations, consolations, or desolations. The reader also gains insight into her life with the sisters. What emerges is an interior life based on trust in God's grace as expressed in the Divine Mercy, a life of simplicity in the presence of God. A constant theme in the *Diary* is the encouraging of sinners to trust in the mercy of God who performs miracles of grace through the Sacrament of Reconciliation: "Persuade all souls to trust in the unfathomable abyss of my mercy because I desire to save them all."

Like other mystics, Sister Faustina passed through the classical dark night of the spirit. Having herself experienced the sufferings of the damned in union with Christ's own redemptive agony, she can recommend trust in God's mercy to souls being "tried as gold in the fire," in order to become "as though just come forth from the [creating] hand of God." With feelings of despair and amid great physical and psychological sufferings, Sister Faustina became ever more aware of God's mysterious pedagogy: "My daughter, if through you I am demanding that people venerate My mercy, then you should be the first to distinguish yourself by trust in My mercy."

TESTIMONY

The testimony of Gather Ignacy Rozycki, a Theologian who studied the life and *Diary* of Sister Faustina, is a wonderful example of how prejudice changed to deep admiration of her. It is quoted in the introduction to a paper he gave at the symposium marking the 50th Anniversary of the revelations to Sister Faustina in Cracow, Poland, February, 1981. It was printed after he died on October 14, 1983.

INTRODUCTION TO THE AUTHOR

The Reverend Professor, Dr. Ignacy Rozycki, was born in 1911 in Kryspinow, in the parish of Liski, near Cracow, Poland. His elementary education took place in his native locality; his secondary schooling, which he completed with distinction, in the St. Ann Grammar-School in Cracow.

In 1930 he entered the Archdiocesan Seminary in Cracow, but shortly thereafter his superiors sent him to Rome, where he studied at the Dominican University called the "Angelicum."

In 1934 he was ordained to the priesthood at the hands of the Metropolitan of Cracow, Adam Stefan Sapieha, after which he returned to Rome to complete his studies.

He returned to Poland with a Doctorate in Dogmatic Theology and, having taught in various colleges, gained a reputation as an eminent theologian. He participated in many meetings of European Theologians and accepted a variety of theological tasks given him by Bishops, as well as Roman Congregations. He was made a Canon of the Chapter of Cracow in 1964, and a Prelate of Honor of His Holiness.

Doctor Rozycki became Professor of Dogmatic Theology at the Jagiellonian University and, when the government of his country suppressed the theological faculty at that ancient institution of learning, he continued in that same capacity at the Pontifical Theological Academy that was established by the Church Authorities to take place of the suppressed theological school. He was known as one of Poland's foremost Thomists and served as a Member of the International Theological Commission.

Upon inauguration of the Informative Process concerning the life and virtues of Sister Faustina Kowalska (October 21, 1965), the Metropolitan of Cracow, Karol Wojtyla, charged the Reverend Doctor Rozycki with the task of preparing a critical analysis of the *Diary* of Sister Faustina and of all her writings. The professor was unwilling to undertake this task and intended to give the Archbishop a negative response, as he admits in the introduction to the elaboration of the *Diary* where he wrote:

> The author of the theological study, which here follows, feels he must confess that — for longer than a quarter of a century — he harbored a deep suspicion both to the heroic sanctity of Faustina, and, above all, with regard to the revelations with which — as she herself assured — she had been favored. He considered himself authorized to think this on account of what he learned from those "who were in the know" concerning the case of Faustina...
>
> In the author's judgment, Faustina, a simple girl, and very pious was nonetheless the victim of hallucinations with an undercurrent of hysteria; consequently, not only were her supposed revelations of hysteria devoid of any religious worth, but at the same time and for the same reasons, the heroicity of her life, a lost cause. This bias provoked a categorical and decided refusal of the author to take part as a theologian-expert in the beatification process of Sister Faustina inaugurated by Karol Wojtyla, the Archbishop of Cracow.

The resoluteness of his negative conviction began to waver when purely human curiosity led the author to leaf through the Diary — well, just to pass the time. His hitherto existing opinion was shaken by this casual reading. After a second, careful, methodical reading, the author came to the conclusion that the cause of

Helen-Faustina was worth the trouble of undertaking a strictly scientific study. [It took him over ten years to complete it! (Translator's Note)]

This latter, already the third in the sequence of time, completely convinced the author that:

> Firstly, the information "of those in the know," which at one time was the basis of his negative stance, was incomplete or inaccurate or false;
>
> Secondly, the sanctity of Faustina is truly heroic, and her revelations bear all the marks of super-natural origin;
>
> Thirdly, the author — having arrived at the highest degree of scientific certitude — has the inescapable obligation of bearing witness to it in writing.
>
> Discharging himself of this task, he offers this fruit of his work to the Infinite and Eternal Incarnate Mercy, to render Him thanks for all graces and to implore the forgiveness of his sins.

As can be seen from the quotation above, the inquiry into the inner life of Sister Faustina completely altered the negative position of the Reverend Professor Ignacy Rozycki towards her person, the revelations, and the forms of devotion to The Divine Mercy as well.

Professor Rozycki became the greatest defender of the devotion to The Divine Mercy and venerator of the Servant of God Sister Faustina, for whose cause he spared neither time nor toil to the last moment of his life. Among other things, the Professor is largely responsible for the Votive Mass of The Divine Mercy, approved for use in Poland in October, 1981.

He died in Cracow on October 14, 1983. (Translated by Father Seraphim Michalenko, M.I.C.).

Addendum: In a telegram to the Theological Academy in Cracow on the occasion of Professor Rozycki's funeral, Pope John Paul II said:

> Today, together with you, I commend his soul to The Divine Mercy, to which, particularily in these last years, he dedicated his work and life.

INTRODUCTION

There is a new interest in the message of God's mercy as revealed to Sister Faustina because of the convergence of a number of publications including the encyclical *Rich in Mercy* by Pope John Paul II, the biography and *Diary of Sr. Faustina,* and the presentation of the docu-drama film *Divine Mercy — No Escape.* Moreover the cause of the beatification of Sister Faustina is proceeding. All this makes the message more accessible to us priests and focuses on the urgency of the message of Divine Mercy.

THE PATTERN OF THE BOOK

This book is a gathering together of what Our Lord said through Sister Faustina to priests, about priests, and of special interest to priests as recorded in her *Diary*. The material is gathered under the following headings:

Words spoken for priests, the message of mercy, the urgency of the message, mercy for all, responding to God's mercy, and the special means of drawing on God's mercy. The special means include the Sacraments of the Eucharist and Reconciliation and the elements of devotion to Divine Mercy: the image, the feast, the novena before the feast, the chaplet and the three o'clock prayer.

Under the title of "the cost of mercy" the excerpts from the *Diary* on Sr. Faustina's sharing on the passion of Christ are gathered together.

An APPENDIX contains some of the words of Sister Faustina on topics of special concern to priests:

On suffering with Christ as victims for the salvation of souls,

On confessors and spiritual directors, and the need of holy and experienced priests.

About priests and their special role,
About her confessor Father Joseph Andrasz, S.J., and
spiritual director Father Michael Sopocko, S.T.D.

THE ESSENTIAL LINK BETWEEN MERCY
AND THE PRIESTHOOD

God loves us with a covenant love, a committed, faithful love, a love that is "fatherly," His love is also tender and compassionate, a "motherly" love. In a word, God is MERCIFUL, God is mercy itself.

Mercy is of the very essence of the redemptive incarnation and the priesthood of Christ. By its very nature his priesthood is a work of mercy based on the covenant of mercy that God made with man. Christ brought God's gift of mercy to man, bringing forgiveness of sin by the sacrifice of his own Body and Blood — as a new and eternal covenant of God's merciful love.

Moreover, God has willed to take us into partnership so that we may cooperate in this work of mercy. By our baptism, and more specifically by our Holy Orders, we are ordained as partners of Christ the one High Priest, Redeemer, and Mediator. Like Mary, the Mother of God and of the Church, we too are cooperators with Christ in the work of redemption and mediation — in this work of mercy. As priests we are ordained to be channels and instruments of the Lord's mercy through the Sacraments of Eucharist and Reconciliation.

The conclusion and consequence of God's covenant of mercy and our partnership in it is that, for priests, devotion to The Divine Mercy is not an option. Devotion to The Divine Mercy is of the very nature of the priesthood. That is the reason for this book: to present to priests the words that Our Lord and Sister Faustina addressed to them about mercy.

DEVOTION TO THE DIVINE MERCY

And what is this devotion? It is not "just another devotion." Rather, it is what devotion ought to be in the root sense of the word — a consecration, a dedication by solemn vow. In this sense the "devotion" to The Divine Mercy is a total commitment to God as Mercy — to be merciful as He is merciful. It is a covenant of mercy.

The objection is easily raised by priests about devotion to the Divine Mercy: "Is this still another devotion? We don't need any more devotions." But I like to respond that this is putting the issue of devotion backwards! This is not <u>our</u> devotion to God, rather it is the other way around. It is <u>God's</u> devotion to you and me. The issue of this devotion is that God is Mercy Itself and wants to have mercy on all (See Rom 11:32).

The devotion was brought into new prominence by the revelations of Our Lord to Sister Faustina, begun in 1931, and continuing until her death in 1938. The message of the Lord is one of mercy. Now is the time to turn to his mercy, while it is the day of mercy, before the day of judgment. The Lord asks especially for trust in his mercy; that we implore his mercy, that we honor his mercy by accepting it, that we proclaim his mercy, and that we be merciful to one another. This is the heart of the Gospel!

Moreover, the Lord gave us, through Sister Faustina, special means of drawing on His mercy in addition to the Sacraments of Eucharist and Reconciliation: an image of The Divine Mercy with the signature "Jesus I Trust in You," a Chaplet of The Divine Mercy, a Feast of The Divine Mercy, prayer at the hour of his dying on the cross. A further description of these elements of the devotion will show how it is a **priestly** devotion.

Pope Leo the Great many years ago directed priests to proclaim God's mercy, saying that we have no choice in the matter:

The priest does not have the right to refrain from preaching about so great a mystery, all the more since there cannot be lacking to him material for discourse on the topic of about which enough is never spoken; and, if in the face of God's glory we do not find ourselves in a position to comment on the works of mercy, still, let us apply our efforts and dedicate our intelligence to the point of exhausting all the possibilities of eloquence' (Sermo I, de Passione).

Pope John Paul II, in the encyclical *Dives in Misericordia* also speaks about proclaiming mercy:

> The Church of our time… must become more particularly and profoundly conscious of the need to **bear witness in her whole mission to God's mercy**, following in the footsteps of the tradition of the Old and the New Covenant, and above all of Jesus Christ himself and his apostles (VII, Introduction).

> …the Church must consider it one of her principle duties — at every stage of history and especially in our modern age — **to proclaim and to introduce in life** the mystery of mercy, supremely revealed in Jesus Christ (#14).

ATTITUDES TOWARD PRIVATE REVELATION

Some priests and laity have problems with private revelations, even with those approved by the Church. The attitude of priests is expressed in such statements as, "Oh, it's only a private revelation." "I don't need another private revelation." "That's not for me." "I have problems with devotions and shrines."

Unfortunately, such attitudes are real obstacles to hearing the word of the Lord and our Lady to this present age.

A clear statement of the Church's attitude toward private revelation was made by Pope John Paul II in his homily at Fatima (May 13, 1982). He quoted the Second Vatican Council and applied it to the Fatima revelations:

> The Church has always taught and continues to proclaim that God's revelation was brought to completion in Jesus Christ, who is the fullness of that revelation, and that "no new public revelation is to be expected before the glorious manifestation of our Lord" (*Dei Verbum* 4). The Church evaluates and judges private revelations by the criterion of conformity with that single Revelation.

> If the Church has accepted the message of Fatima, it is above all because the message contains a truth and a call whose basic content is the truth and the call of the Gospel itself.

> "Repeat, and believe in the Gospel" (Lk 1:15): these are the first words that the Messiah addressed to humanity. The message of Fatima is, in its basic nucleus, a call to conversion and repentance, as in the Gospel.

In a few sentences, John Paul II outlined the place of private revelations — they are a **truth and a call of the gospel**. Pope John Paul II's words and actions are clear and strong, but I think other considerations are also helpful.

God did not stop speaking to His people with the death of the last apostle, John the beloved disciple. Public revelation was completed with John's death, but God continues to speak to us today and to give us assurance of his victory. The question is: **Who is listening?**

Here are some other reasons to help appreciate the words of private revelations more fully:

* God is free. He can speak to us if he wants. God has something important to say to us.
* Private revelations are historical facts.
* They confirm the Gospel.
* They give a current emphasis to truths of faith and morals.
* They give guidance in choosing a path in times of crisis.
* The content of the message is rich for upbuilding our faith.

Another consideration is the realization that private revelations are among the charisms that the Second Vatican Council encouraged: "These charismatic gifts, whether they be the most outstanding or the more simple and widely diffused, are to be received with thanksgiving and consolation, for they are exceedingly suitable and useful for the needs of the Church" (*Lumen Gentium,* 12).

Bishop Graber of Regensburg, addressing the Fatima Congress at Freiburg, Germany, September 23, 1973, gave a moving talk on the question of private revelation:

Once again we affirm that revelation ended with Christ and His Apostles. But does that mean that God has to remain silent, that He can no longer speak to His elect? Does it mean, as some believers think, that He should remain apart and leave the world abandoned to itself? Would not this be a very strange kind of God indeed! Did He not expressly say through His prophet that He would "pour forth of His Spirit on all flesh, that sons and daughters would prophesy, that old men would have visions in dreams. Even upon servants and handmaids He would pour forth of His Spirit" (Acts 2:17; Jn 3:1-5). Is such prophecy to be limited only to the first Pentecost? Certainly not (Quoted in *Fatima: The Great Sign*, Francis Johnston, A.M.I., Washington, N.J., 07882).

St. Thomas Aquinas writing on prophecy says:

As regards the direction of human acts, prophetic revelation was diversified not according to the process of time, but according to the needs of circumstances; because, as is said in Proverbs, "Where there is no prophecy, the people cast off restraint" (29:18). That is why at every period men were instructed by God about what they were to do, according as was expedient for the salvation of the elect.

And again in the same article:

At each period there were always some who had the spirit of prophecy, not for the purpose of setting out new doctrine to be believed, but for the governance of human activities (*Summa II,II,Q.*176,a.6).

In the article "Theology of Devotion to the Sacred Heart," found in *Theological Investigations* (Vol. III, pp. 338, 339). Father Karl Rahner, S.J., explains that, while private revelations do not offer new doctrine for belief, they do provide extraordinary guidance for the Church, emphasizing specific and urgent ways of putting faith into action. They present us with God's evaluation of what is most needed at particular times.

To this, Father Walter Kern, in his *Updated Devotion to the Sacred Heart,* adds an important consideration. He explains that private revelations.

...are offered as a special grace for the good of men in general. One can save his or her soul without every special grace from God, but the fact that God offered it, because it is or was useful, must weigh heavily in one's judgment of it.

XX

Especially in times of travail, like ours, we need to hear the word of the Lord proclaimed clearly and forcefully like a clear trumpet. "If the bugle's sound is uncertain, who will get ready for the battle?' (1 Cor 14:8). Who will be able to listen and act? Who will be able to say with Samuel, "Speak, Lord for your servant is listening" (1 Sm 3:9)?

Chapter I

WORDS SPOKEN FOR PRIESTS

On five occasions our Lord told Sister Faustina to tell priests about his mercy. She was to tell them:

* that they are to receive mercy (177),
* that they are to tell everyone about his great and unfathomable mercy (570),
* that they are to proclaim mercy to sinners (50),
* that hardened sinners will repent on hearing their words of mercy, and wondrous power to touch hearts will be given to priests who proclaim his mercy (1521), and
* that priests are to recommend the chaplet of The Divine Mercy to sinners (687).

Our Lady also addressed priests through Sister Faustina (See 1585).

WORDS OF CHRIST TO PRIESTS

On proclaiming and preaching mercy, especially to sinners:

50   **"I desire that priests proclaim this great mercy of Mine** towards souls of sinners. Let the sinner not be afraid to approach Me. The flames of mercy are burning Me — clamoring to be spent; I want to pour them out upon these souls."

177   And again Jesus said to me with kindness, "My daughter, **speak to priests about this inconceivable mercy of Mine.** The flames of mercy are burning Me — clamoring to be spent; I want to keep pouring them out upon souls; souls just don't want to believe in My goodness."

570   "No soul will be justified until it turns with confidence to My mercy, and this is why the first Sunday after Easter is to be the Feast of Mercy. On that day, **priests are to tell everyone about My great and unfathomable mercy.** I am making you the administrator of My mercy. **Tell the confessor** that the Image is to be on view in the church and not within the enclosure in that convent. By means of this Image I shall be granting many graces to souls; so, let every soul have access to it.

1521   The Lord said to me, "My daughter, do not tire of proclaiming My mercy. In this way you will refresh this Heart of Mine, which burns with a flame of pity for sinners. **Tell My priests that hardened sinners will repent on hearing their words when they speak about My unfathomable mercy,** about the compassion I have for them in My Heart. **To priests who will proclaim and extol My mercy, I will give wondrous power; I will anoint their words and touch the hearts of those to whom they will speak.**"

On recommending the Chaplet:

687   Once, as I was going down the hall to the kitchen, I heard these words in my soul:"Say unceasingly the chaplet that I have taught you. Whoever will recite it will receive great mercy at the hour of death. **Priests will recommend it to sinners as their last hope of salvation.** Even if there were a sinner most hardened, if he were to recite this chaplet only once, he would receive grace from My infinite mercy. I desire that the whole world know My infinite mercy. I desire to grant unimaginable graces to those souls who trust in My mercy."

WORDS OF OUR LADY TO PRIESTS

1585 A vision of the Mother of God. In the midst of a great brilliance, I saw the Mother of God clothed in a white gown, girt about with a golden cincture; and there were tiny stars, also of gold, over the whole garment, and chevron-shaped sleeves lined with gold. Her cloak was sky-blue, lightly thrown over the shoulders. A transparent veil was delicately drawn over her head, while her flowing hair was set off beautifully by a golden crown which terminated in little crosses. On Her left arm She held the Child Jesus. A Blessed Mother of this type I had not yet seen. Then She looked at me kindly and said: ***"I am the Mother of God of Priests."*** At that, She lowered Jesus from Her arm to the ground, raised Her right hand heavenward and said: "O God, bless Poland, bless priests." Then She addressed me once again: ***"Tell the priests what you have seen."*** I resolved that at the first opportunity [I would have] of seeing Father [Andrasz] I would tell; but I myself can make nothing of this vision.

• In Polish: "Jestem Matka Boska Kaplanska." Literally: "I am the Mother of God of Priests." or equivalently: "I am the Theotokos of Priests."

THE GOSPEL VALIDITY OF THE MESSAGES

The six messages of Our Lord and Our Lady addressed to Sister Faustina in regard to priests are entirely in keeping with Pope John Paul II's criterion for acceptable private revelations. They contain "a truth and a call whose basic content is the truth and call of the gospel itself" (*Homily at Fatima,* 1982).

This gospel dimension of the messages can be most clearly seen by reexamining each message, isolating a few key words that summarize its basic content, and then comparing these key words to some of the many texts of the *Old* and *New* Testament that speak of trust in God and of his mercy.

"I desire that priests proclaim this great mercy of Mine towards souls of sinners. Let the sinner not be afraid to approach Me. The flames of mercy are burning Me — clamoring to be spent; I want to pour them out upon these souls." (*Diary* 50).

Key Words:

* Preach his great mercy
* Reach out to sinners
* Tell them of his desire to be merciful

Mt 4:17   *"From that time on Jesus began to proclaim this theme: 'Reform your lives! The kingdom of God is at hand.'"*

Mt 11:28-30   *"Come to me, all you who are weary and I will refresh you. Take my yoke upon your shoulders and learn from me, for I am gentle and humble of heart. Your souls will find rest, for my yoke is easy and my burden light."*

Lk 6:36   *"Be compassionate as your Father is compassionate."*

Jn 19-28   *"I am thirsty."*

Rom 10:12b-15b   All have the same Lord, rich in mercy towards all who call upon him. *"Everyone who calls on the name of the Lord will be saved."* But how shall they call on him in *whom they have not believed? And how can they believe unless they have heard of him? And how can they hear unless there is someone to preach? And how can men preach unless they are sent?*

Lk 15:32   **Prodigal Son** — *"But we had to celebrate and rejoice! This brother of yours was dead, and has come back to life. He was lost, and is found."*

"My daughter, *speak to priests about this inconceivable mercy of Mine.* The flames of mercy are burning Me — clamoring to be spent; I want to keep pouring them out upon souls; souls just don't want to believe in My goodness" (*Diary* 177).

Key Words:

* Priests themselves need to know his mercy and trust him.

Jn 13:1   *He loved his own in this world, and would show his love for them to the end* [utmost].

Jn 15:13   *"There is no greater love than this: to lay down one's life for one's friends."*

Jn 15:15   *"...I call you friends since I have made known to you all that I heard from my Father."*

"No soul will be justified until it turns with confidence to My mercy, and this is why the first Sunday after Easter is to be the Feast of Mercy. On that day, priests are to tell everyone about My great and unfathomable mercy. I am making you the administrator of My mercy. Tell the

confessor that the image is to be on view in the church and not within the enclosure in that convent. By means of this image I shall be granting many graces to souls; so let everyone have access to it" (*Diary* 570).

Key Words:

* Souls need mercy for salvation.

* The feast of mercy is a day of forgiveness and atonement.

* Priests are to tell **everyone** of his great mercy.

* The image of The Divine Mercy (Jesus with his hand raised in blessing) is a vessel of grace.

Gal 2:20b   *[He] loved me and gave himself for me.*

2Cor 5:14-15   *The love of Christ impels us who have reached the conviction that since one died for all, all died. He died for all so that those who live might live no longer for themselves, but for him who for their sake died and was raised up.*

Jn 20:19 23   *On the evening of that first day of the week, even though the disciples had locked the doors of the place where they were for fear of the Jews, Jesus came and stood before them. "Peace be with you," he said. When he had said this, he showed them his hands and side. At the sight of the Lord the disciples rejoiced. "Peace be with you," he said again. "As the Father has sent me, so I send you." Then he breathed on them and said: "Receive the Holy Spirit. If you forgive men's sins, they are forgiven them; if you hold them bound, they are bound."*

Sir 50:14-21   *(Simon, the high priest, on the day of atonement:)*

Once he had completed the services at the altar with the arranging of the sacrifices for the Most High, and had stretched forth his hand for the cup, to offer blood of the grape, and poured it out at the foot of the altar... The sons of Aaron would sound a blast... as a reminder before the Most High. Then all the people with one accord would quickly fall prostrate to the ground in adoration before the Most High, before the Holy One of Israel.... All the people of the land would shout for joy, praying to the Merciful One, ...Then coming down he [the high priest] would raise his hands over the congregation of Israel. The blessing of the Lord would be upon his lips, the name of the Lord [Yahweh] would be his glory. Then again the people would lie prostrate to receive from him the blessing of the Most High.

Lk 24:50-52   *Then he led them out near Bethany, and with his hands upraised, blessed them. As he blessed them, he left them, and was taken up to heaven. They fell down to do him reverence.*

Acts 3:26   *When God raised up his servant, he sent him first to bless you by turning you from your evil ways.*

"Say unceasingly the chaplet that I have taught you. Whoever will recite it will receive great mercy at the hour of death. Priests will recommend it to sinners as their last hope of salvation. Even if there were a sinner most hardened, if he recites this chaplet only once, he will receive

8

grace from My infinite mercy. I desire that the whole
world know My infinite mercy. I desire to grant
unimaginable graces to those souls who trust in My
mercy" (*Diary* 687).

Key Words:

* Pray the chaplet

* Recommend the chaplet
    to the dying
    to sinners

* He wants the whole world
    to know
    to receive
    to trust in—His Infinite Mercy

* Words of the chaplet:

> Eternal Father, I offer you the Body and Blood,
> Soul and Divinity of Your Dearly Beloved Son, Our
> Lord, Jesus Christ, in atonement for our sins and
> those of the whole world.

> For the sake of His sorrowful Passion, have
> mercy on us and on the whole world.

> Holy God, Holy Mighty One, Holy Immortal
> One, have mercy on us and on the whole world.

1Jn 2:2
> *He is an offering [atonement] for our sins,
> and not for our sins only, but for those of the
> whole world.*

1Cor 10:16
> *Is not the cup of blessing we bless a
> sharing in the blood of Christ? And is not
> the bread we break a sharing in the body
> of Christ?.*

Is 6:3 — *"Holy, holy, holy is the Lord of Hosts!" they cried one to another. "All the earth is filled with his glory!'*

Is 57:15 — *For thus says he who is high and exalted, living eternally, whose name is the Holy One: On high I dwell, and in holiness, and with the crushed and dejected in spirit, to revive the spirits of the rejected, to revive the hearts of the crushed.*

1Pt 2:5 — *You too are living stones, built as an edifice of spirit, into a holy priesthood, offering spiritual sacrifices acceptable to God through Jesus Christ.*

Heb 13:15-16 — *Through him let us continually offer God a sacrifice of praise, that is, the fruit of lips which acknowledge his name. Do not neglect good deeds and generosity: God is pleased by sacrifices of that kind.*

Heb 13:20-21 — *May the God of peace, who brought up from the dead the great Shepherd of the sheep by the blood of the eternal covenant, Jesus Christ our Lord, furnish you with all that is good, that you may do his will.*

Heb 4:16 — *So let us confidently approach the throne of grace to receive mercy and favor and find help in time of need.*

Mt 5:7 — *"Blest are they that show mercy; mercy shall be theirs."*

Mt 6:33 — *"Seek first his kingship over you, his way of holiness, and all these things will be given you besides."*

Lk 12:32-34 — *"Do not live in fear, little flock. It has pleased your Father to give you the*

*kingdom. Sell what you have and give alms...
Wherever your treasure lies, there your heart
will be."*

Eph 2:4-5

*"God is rich in mercy; because of his great
love for us he brought us to life with Christ
when we were dead in sin."*

2Cor 1:3-4

*Praised be God the Father of our Lord Jesus
Christ, the Father of mercies, and the God of
all consolation! He comforts us in all our
afflictions and thus enables us to comfort
those who are in trouble, with the same consolation we have received from him.*

2Cor 1:9-11

*We were left to feel like men condemned to
death so that we might trust, not in ourselves,
but in God who raised the dead. He rescued
us from the danger of death and will
continue to do so. We have put our hope in
him who will never cease to deliver us. But
you must help us with your prayers, so that
on our behalf God may be thanked for
the gifts granted us through the prayers of
so many.*

Rom 11:32-36

*God has imprisoned all in disobedience that
he might have mercy on all. How deep are
the riches and the wisdom of God! How
inscrutable his judgments, how unsearchable
his ways! For "who has been his counselor?
Who has given him anything so as to deserve
return?" For from him and for him all things
are. To him be glory forever. Amen.*

**"Tell My priests that hardened sinners will repent on hear-
ing their words, when they speak about My unfathomable
mercy, about the compassion I have for them in My Heart.**

To priests who will proclaim and extol My mercy, I will give wondrous power, and I will anoint their words and touch the hearts of those to whom they will speak" (*Diary* 1521).

Key Words:

* Glorify his mercy
* Proclaim his mercy
* Wondrous power will be given
* Hearts will be opened

Mk 6:12-13   *With that they went off, preaching the need of repentance. They expelled many demons, anointed the sick with oil, and worked many cures.*

Jn 14:12   *"I solemnly assure you, the man who has faith in me will do the works I do and greater than these."*

Acts 2:37-38   *When they heard this, they were deeply shaken. They asked Peter and the other apostles, "What are we to do brothers?" Peter answered: "You must reform and be baptized, each one of you. in the name of Jesus Christ, that your sins may be forgiven; then you will receive the gift of the Holy Spirit."*

Acts 3:6-8   *Then Peter said: "I have neither silver nor gold but what I have I give you! In the name of Jesus Christ, the Nazorean, walk!" Then Peter took him by the right hand and pulled him up. Immediately the begger's feet and ankles became strong; he jumped up, stood*

12

up for a moment, then began to walk around. He went into the temple with them — walking, jumping about, and giving praise to God.

A vision of the Mother of God. In the midst of a great brilliance, I saw the Mother of God clothed in a white gown, girt about with a golden cincture; and there were tiny stars, also of gold, over the whole garment, and chevron-shaped sleeves lined with gold. Her cloak was sky-blue, lightly thrown over the shoulders. A transparent veil was delicately drawn over her head, while her flowing hair was set off beautifully by a golden crown which terminated in little crosses. On Her left arm She held the Child Jesus. A Blessed Mother of this type I had not yet seen. Then She looked at me kindly and said, "I am the Mother-of-God of Priests." At that, She lowered Jesus from Her arm to the ground, raised Her right hand heavenward and said: "O God, bless Poland, bless priests." Then She addressed me once again: "Tell the priests what you have seen." I resolved that at the very first opportunity [I would have] of seeing Father [Andrasz] I would tell; but I myself can make nothing of this vision (*Diary* 1585).

Key Words:

* Mary is Mother of God and our mother
* Be witnesses of what you have seen

Jn 19:26-27
Seeing his mother there with the disciple whom he loved, Jesus said to his mother, "Woman, there is your son." In turn he said to his disciple, "There is your mother." From that hour onward, the disciple took her into his care.

Jn 19:34
One of the soldiers thrust a lance into his side, and immediately **blood and water** *flowed out.*

This testimony has been given by an eye witness, and his testimony is true. He tells what he knows is true, so that you may believe.

Lk 1:49-50

"God who is mighty has done great things for me, holy is his name; His mercy is from age to age on those who fear him."

Acts 1:14

Together they devoted themselves to constant prayer. There were some women in their company, and Mary the mother of Jesus and his brothers.

In regard to the stars on our Lady's robe:

Dn 12:3

But the wise shall shine brightly like the splendor of the firmament, and those who lead the many to justice shall be like the stars forever.

Ps 45:10

The queen stands at your right hand arrayed in cloth of gold (Queenship of Mary. Entrance Antiphon).

Chapter II

THE MESSAGE OF MERCY

Mercy is what we, as priests, are to preach. God's merciful love is greater than all sin, greater than all evil and greater than death itself. Mercy is the greatest attribute of God — it is his love poured out on us sinners. No matter what we have done God wants us to repent and turn to His mercy with trust. Everyone needs to hear the message of God's Mercy.

The *Diary* is filled with references to mercy — a complete teaching on mercy. Focusing on some of the strongest words of Our Lord can help us, as priests, to understand and so proclaim with greater urgency the depths of his desire to have mercy on us.

* In the material to follow from the Diary of Sister Faustina the number in the margin is the point of reference in the Diary of Sister Faustina. The emphasis is added by the compiler.

180 The third attribute is love and mercy. And I understood that the **greatest attribute is love and mercy**. It unites the creature with the Creator. This immense love and abyss of mercy are made known in the Incarnation of the Word and in the Redemption [of humanity], and it is here that I saw this as the greatest of all God's attributes.

186 **I desire that you know more profoundly the love that burns in My Heart for souls,** and you will understand this when you meditate upon My Passion. Call upon My mercy on behalf of sinners; I desire their salvation. When you say this prayer, with a contrite heart and with faith on behalf of some sinner, I will give him the grace of conversion.

187   **This is the prayer:**
      "O Blood and Water, which gushed forth from the Heart of Jesus as a fount of Mercy for us, I trust in You."

300   +Mankind will not have peace until it turns with trust to My mercy.

      "My Heart rejoices in this title of Mercy."

301   **"Proclaim that mercy is the greatest attribute of God. All the works of My hands are crowned with mercy."**

359   January 10, 1935. +Thursday. In the evening during benediction, such thoughts as these began to distress me: Is not perhaps all this that I am saying about God's great mercy just a lie or an illusion...? And I wanted to think about this for a while, when I heard a strong and clear inner voice saying, **"Everything that you say about My goodness is true; language has no adequate expression to extol My goodness."** These words were so filled with power and so clear that I would give my life in declaring they came from God. I can tell this by the profound peace that accompanied them at that time and that still remains with me. This peace gives me such great strength and power that all difficulties, adversities, sufferings, and death itself are as nothing. This light gave me a glimpse of the truth that all my efforts to bring souls to know the mercy of the Lord are very pleasing to God. And from this springs such great joy in my soul that I do not know whether it could be any greater in heaven. Oh, if souls would only be willing to listen, at least a little, to the voice of conscience and the voice — that is, the inspirations — of the Holy Spirit! I say "at least a little," because once we open ourselves to the influence of the Holy Spirit, He Himself will fulfill what is lacking in us.

528   On Friday, during Mass, when my soul was flooded with God's happiness, I heard these words in my soul: **"My mercy has passed into souls through the divine-human Heart of Jesus** as a ray from the sun passes through crystal." I felt in my heart and understood that every approach to God is brought about by Jesus, in Him and through Him.

723   + Today, I heard these words: "The graces I grant you are not for you alone, but for a great number of other souls as well... And your heart is My constant dwelling place, despite the misery that you are. I unite Myself with you, take away your misery and give you My mercy. I perform works of mercy in every soul. **The greater the sinner, the greater the right he has to My mercy.** My mercy is confirmed in every work of My hands. **He who trusts in My mercy will not perish,** for all his affairs are Mine, and his enemies will be shattered at the base of My footstool."

998   Today, I took part in a one-day retreat. When I was at the last conference, the priest was speaking of how much the world needs God's mercy, and that this seems to be a special time when people have great need of prayer and God's mercy. Then I heard a voice in my soul: "These words are for you. Do all you possibly can for this work of My mercy. **I desire that My mercy be worshiped,** and I am giving mankind the last hope of salvation; that is, recourse to My mercy. My Heart rejoices in this feast. After these words, I understood that nothing can dispense me from the obligation which the Lord demands from me.

1074   When I went for adoration, I heard these words: "My beloved daughter, write down these words, that today My Heart has rested in this convent. **Tell the world about My mercy and My love.**

       "The flames of mercy are burning me. I desire to pour them out upon human souls. Oh, what

18

pain they cause Me when they do not want to accept them!

"My daughter, do whatever is within your power to spread devotion to My mercy. I will make up for what you lack. Tell aching mankind to snuggle close to My merciful Heart, and I will fill it with peace.

"Tell [all people], My daughter, that **I am Love and Mercy itself** When a soul approaches Me with trust, I fill it with such an abundance of graces that it cannot contain them within itself, **but radiates them to other souls.**

1075 **"Souls who spread the honor of My mercy I shield through their entire lives as a tender mother her infant,** and at the hour of death I will not be a Judge for them, but the Merciful Savior. At that last hour, a soul has nothing with which to defend itself except My mercy. Happy is the soul that during its lifetime immersed itself in the Fountain of Mercy, because justice will have no hold on it.

1076 "Write this: **Everything that exists is enclosed in the bowels of My mercy, more deeply than an infant in its mother's womb.** How painfully distrust of My goodness wounds Me! Sins of distrust wound Me most painfully."

1142 June 4. Today is the Feast of the Most Sacred Heart of Jesus. During Holy Mass, I was given the knowledge of the Heart of Jesus and of the nature of the fire of love with which He burns for us and of how He is an Ocean of Mercy. Then I heard a voice: "**Apostle of My mercy, proclaim to the whole world My unfathomable mercy.** Do not be discouraged by the difficulties you encounter in proclaiming My mercy. These difficulties that affect you so painfully are needed for your sanctification and as evidence that this work is Mine. My daughter, be diligent in writing down every sentence I tell you concerning My mercy, because this is meant for a great number of souls who will profit from it."

1190 + Jesus. — "From all My wounds, like from streams, mercy flows for souls, but **the wound in My heart is the fountain of unfathomable mercy.** From this fountain spring all graces for souls. The flames of compassion burn Me. I desire greatly to pour them out upon souls. Speak to the whole world about My mercy."

1273 Jesus: "My daughter, do you think you have written enough about My mercy? **What you have written is but a drop compared to the ocean. I am Love and Mercy Itself.** There is no misery that could be a match for My mercy, neither will misery exhaust it, because as it is being granted — it increases. The soul that trusts in My mercy is most fortunate, because I Myself take care of it."

1516 "My daughter, **tell souls that I am giving them My mercy as a defense.** I Myself am fighting for them and am bearing the just anger of My Father."

1576 "Know, My daughter, that between Me and you there is a bottomless abyss, an abyss which separates the Creator from the creature. **But this abyss is filled with My mercy.** I raise you up to Myself, not that I have need of you, but it is solely out of mercy that I grant you the grace of union with Myself."

1577 "Tell souls not to place within their own hearts obstacles to My mercy, which so greatly wants to act within them. **My mercy works in all those hearts which open their doors to it.** Both the sinner as well as the righteous person have need of My mercy. Conversion, as well as perseverance, is a grace of My mercy."

1667   Holy Saturday. During Adoration, the Lord said to me, "Be at peace, My daughter. **This Work of mercy is Mine;** there is nothing of you in it. It pleases Me that you are carrying out faithfully what I have commanded you to do, not adding or taking away a single word." And He gave me an interior light by which **I learned that not a single word was mine;** despite difficulties and adversities, I have always, always, fulfilled His will, as He has made it known to me.

1739   "Write, My daughter, that **I am mercy itself for the contrite soul.** A soul's greatest wretchedness does not enkindle Me with wrath; but rather, My Heart is moved towards it with great mercy."

1777   +Conference on mercy.

"My daughter, know that **My Heart is mercy itself.** From this sea of mercy, graces flow out upon the whole world. No soul that has approached Me has ever gone away unconsoled. **All misery gets buried in the depths of My mercy,** and every saving and sanctifying grace flows from this fountain. My daughter, I desire that your heart be an abiding place of My mercy. I desire that this mercy flow out upon the whole world through your heart. Let no one who approaches you go away without that trust in My mercy which I so ardently desire for souls. Pray as much as you can for the dying. By your entreaties, obtain for them trust in My mercy, because they have most need of trust, and have it the least. Be assured that the grace of eternal salvation for certain souls in their final moment depends on your prayer. You know the whole abyss of My mercy, so draw upon it for yourself and especially for poor sinners. Sooner would heaven and earth turn into nothingness than would My mercy not embrace a trusting soul.

Chapter III

THE URGENCY OF THE MESSAGE

There is an urgency about proclaiming the mercy of the Lord because now is the day of mercy before the coming of the day of judgment. Now is the time to prepare for the coming of the Lord. There is a special urgency in the very message of mercy as related by Our Lord and Our Lady to Sister Faustina. As priests, it is important that we look at these words for the sake of our people.

83   "Write this: **before I come as the Just Judge, I am coming first as the King of Mercy.** Before the day of justice arrives, there will be given to people a **sign in the heavens** of this sort:

     "All light in the heavens will be extinguished, and there will be great darkness over the whole earth. Then the sign of the cross will be seen in the sky, and from the openings where the hands and the feet of the Savior were nailed will come forth great lights which will light up the earth for a period of time. This will take place shortly before the last day."

635   March 25th. In the morning, during meditation, God's presence enveloped me in a special way, as I saw the immeasurable greatness of God and, at the same time, His condescension to His creatures. Then I saw the Mother of God, who said to me, "Oh, how pleasing to God is the soul that follows faithfully the inspirations of His grace! I gave the Savior to the world; as for you, you have to speak to the world about His great mercy and prepare the world for the Second Coming of Him who will come, not as a merciful Savior, but as a just Judge. Oh, how terrible is that day! Determined is the day of justice, the day of divine wrath. The angels tremble

before it. Speak to souls about this great mercy while it is still the time for [granting] mercy. If you keep silent now, you will be answering for a great number of souls on that terrible day. Fear nothing. Be faithful to the end. I sympathize with you."

848 "...Write down these words, My daughter. Speak to the world about My mercy; let all mankind recognize My unfathomable mercy. **It is a sign for the end times;** after it will come the day of justice. **While there is still time, let them have recourse to the fount of My mercy;** let them profit from the Blood and Water which gushed forth for them."

O human souls, where are you going to hide on the day of God's anger: Take refuge now in the fount of God's mercy. O what a great multitude of souls I see! They worshiped the Divine Mercy and will be singing the hymn of praise for all eternity.

1159 **God's floodgates have been opened for us. Let us want to take advantage of them before the day of God's justice arrives.** And that will be a dreadful day!

1160 When once I asked the Lord Jesus how He could tolerate so many sins and crimes and not punish them, the Lord answered me, "I have eternity for punishing [these], and so **I am prolonging the time of mercy for the sake of [sinners].** But woe to them if they do not recognize this time of My visitation. My daughter, secretary of My mercy, your duty is not only to write about and proclaim My mercy, but also to beg for this grace for them, so that they too may glorify My mercy."

1588 Today I heard the words: "In the Old Covenant I sent prophets wielding thunderbolts to My people. Today I am sending you with My mercy to the people of the whole world. I do not want to punish aching mankind, but I desire to heal it, pressing it to My Merciful Heart. I use punishment when they themselves force Me to do so; My hand is reluctant to take hold of the sword of justice. Before the Day of Justice I am sending the Day of Mercy." I replied, "O my Jesus, speak to souls Yourself, because my words are insignificant."

Chapter IV

MERCY FOR ALL

To whom is mercy proclaimed? To all, especially the greatest sinners. The Lord wants to have mercy on us all (Rom 11, 32), but he can only have mercy on those who are open to his mercy; that is, the humble. All of us sinners need to call upon his mercy, turn to his mercy and receive his mercy. The Lord's words to Sister Faustina are a strong call to pray for sinners and to proclaim his mercy by preaching, teaching and writing. To contrite souls Jesus is mercy itself.

The Lord pleads with us to reach out to sinners — to help them to repent and to turn to the mercy of the Lord. The Lord delights in the repentence of each sinner — and waits, not with anger, but with his compassionate mercy.

As priests, we bring this good news of God's mercy to so many miserable souls in need.

206   The next day, after Communion, I heard the voice saying, "My daughter, look into the abyss of My mercy and give praise and glory to this mercy of Mine. Do it in this way: Gather all sinners from the entire world and immerse them in the abyss of My mercy. I want to give Myself to souls; I yearn for souls, My daughter. On the day of My feast, the Feast of Mercy, you will go through the whole world and bring fainting souls to the spring of My mercy. I shall heal and strengthen them."

378   But God has promised a great grace especially to you and to all those... "who will proclaim My great mercy. I shall protect them Myself at the hour of death, as My own glory. **And even if the sins of soul are as dark as night, when the sinner turns to My mercy, he gives Me**

the greatest praise and is the glory of My Passion. When a soul praises My goodness, Satan trembles before it and flees to the very bottom of hell.

1146 "[Let] the greatest sinners place their trust in My mercy. They have the right before others to trust in the abyss of My mercy. My daughter, write about My mercy towards tormented souls. Souls that make an appeal to My mercy delight Me. To such souls I grant even more graces than they ask. I cannot punish even the greatest sinner if he makes an appeal to My compassion, but on the contrary, I justify him in My unfathomable and inscrutable mercy. Write: before I come as a just Judge, I first open wide the door of My mercy. He who refuses to pass through the door of My mercy must pass through the door of My justice..."

1182 + Today the Lord said to me, "My daughter, My pleasure and delight, nothing will stop Me from granting you graces. Your misery does not hinder My mercy. My daughter, write that the greater the misery of a soul, the greater its right to My mercy; [urge] all souls to trust in the unfathomable abyss of My mercy, because I want to save them all. On the Cross, the fountain of My mercy was opened wide by the lance for all souls — no one have I excluded!"

1275 My Secretary, write that I am more generous toward sinners than toward the just. It was for their sake that I came down from heaven; it was for their sake that My Blood was spilled. Let them not fear to approach Me; they are most in need of My mercy."

1396 Today I heard a voice in my soul: "Oh, if sinners knew My mercy, they would not perish in such great numbers. Tell sinful souls not to be afraid to approach Me; speak to them of My great mercy."

1397   The Lord said to me, **"The loss of each soul plunges Me into mortal sadness. You always console Me when you pray for sinners. The prayer most pleasing to Me is prayer for the conversion of sinners. Know, My daughter, that this prayer is always heard and answered."**

1485   Conversation of the Merciful God with a Sinful Soul.

     Jesus: **"Be not afraid of your Savior, O sinful soul.** I make the first move to come to you, for I know that by yourself you are unable to lift yourself to me. Child, do not run away from your Father; be willing to talk openly with your God of mercy who wants to speak words of pardon and lavish his graces on you. How dear your soul is to Me! I have inscribed your name upon My hand; you are engraved as a deep wound in My Heart."

1520   Today the Lord said to me, **"I have opened My Heart as a living fountain of mercy.** Let all souls draw life from it. Let them approach this sea of mercy with great trust. **Sinners will attain justification,** and the just will be confirmed in good. Whoever places his trust in My mercy will be filled with My divine peace at the hour of death.

1521   The Lord said to me, "My daughter, do not tire of proclaiming My mercy. In this way you will refresh this Heart of Mine, which burns with a flame of pity for sinners.

1665   During Holy Hour in the evening, I heard the words, **"You see My mercy for sinners,** which at this moment is revealing itself in all its power. See how little you have written about it; it is only a single drop. Do what is in your power, so that sinners may come to know My goodness."

1666   Good Friday, I saw the Lord Jesus, tortured, but not nailed to the Cross. It was still before the crucifixion, and He said to me, "You are My Heart. Speak to **sinners about My mercy**." And the Lord gave me interior knowledge of the whole abyss of His mercy for souls, and I learned that that which I had written is truly a drop.

1728   Write: I am Thrice Holy, and I detest the smallest sin. **I cannot love a soul which is stained with sin; but when it repents, there is no limit to My generosity toward it. My mercy embraces and justifies it.** With My mercy, I pursue sinners along all their paths, and My Heart rejoices when they return to Me. I forget the bitterness with which they fed My Heart and rejoice at their return. Tell sinners that no one shall escape My Hand; if they run away from My merciful Heart, they will fall into My just hands. **Tell sinners that I am always waiting for them,** that I listen intently to the beating of their heart... when will it beat for Me? Write, that I am speaking to them through their remorse of conscience, through their failures and sufferings, through thunderstorms, through the voice of the Church. And if they bring all My graces to naught, I begin to be angry with them, leaving them alone and giving them what they want."

1739   "Write, My daughter, that I am mercy itself for the contrite soul. **A soul's greatest wretchedness does not enkindle Me with wrath; but rather, My Heart is moved towards it with great mercy.**"

Chapter V

RESPONDING TO GOD'S MERCY

How are we to respond to God's mercy? By trusting in the Lord and by being merciful — these are the fundamental ways.

TRUST in the Lord is the fundamental way of responding to and acknowledging the Lord's mercy and of thanking him. To trust is to place our whole lives in the merciful hands of the Lord with confidence — He is Lord and he loves us and cares for us. Trust is the vessel to draw mercy.

BE MERCIFUL as I am merciful" — in words, deeds and prayer. This is the fundamental way of expressing our trust in him — by **word** in preaching, teaching and writing we let others know of God's mercy; by **deeds** we show others how to be merciful; by **prayer** we implore mercy for sinners and glorify the mercy of the Lord.

As priests, we need to grow in trust in the Lord and so lead fearful souls to trust in His mercy, and be merciful.

50   Jesus complained to me in these words, "**Distrust on the part of souls is tearing at My insides.** The distrust of a chosen soul causes Me even greater pain; despite My inexhaustible love for them they do not trust Me. Even My death is not enough for them. Woe to the soul that abuses these [gifts]!"

687   "I desire to grant unimaginable graces to those souls **who trust in My mercy**."

300   +"Oh, how much **I am hurt by a soul's distrust!** Such a soul professes that I am Holy and Just, but does not believe that I am Mercy and does not trust in My Goodness. Even the devils glorify My Justice but do not believe in My Goodness."

379   During one of the adorations, Jesus promised me that:

With souls that have recourse to My mercy and with those that glorify and proclaim My great mercy to others, I will deal according to My infinite mercy at the hour of their death.

"My Heart is sorrowful," Jesus said, "because **even chosen souls do not understand the greatness of My mercy.** Their relationship [with Me] is, in certain ways, imbued with mistrust. Oh, how much that wounds My Heart! Remember My Passion, and if you do not believe My words, at least believe My wounds."

742   My daughter, if I demand through you that people revere My mercy, you should be the first to distinguish yourself by this confidence in My mercy. I demand from you deeds of mercy, which are to arise out of love for Me. You are to show mercy to your neighbors always and everywhere. You must not shrink from this or try to excuse or absolve yourself from it.

I am giving you three ways of exercising mercy toward your neighbor: the first — by deed, the second **— by word,** the third — **by prayer.** In these three degrees is contained the fullness of mercy, and it is an unquestionable proof of love for Me. By this means a soul glorifies and pays reverence to My mercy. Yes, the first Sunday after Easter is the Feast of Mercy, but there must also be acts of mercy, and I demand the worship of My mercy through the solemn celebration of the Feast and through the veneration of the image which is painted. By means of this image I shall grant many graces to souls. It is to be a reminder of the demands of My mercy, because even the strongest faith is of no avail without works."

1148   "Every soul, and especially the soul of every religious, should reflect My mercy. My Heart overflows with compassion and mercy for all. **The heart of My beloved must resemble Mine;** from her heart must spring the fountain of My mercy for souls; otherwise I will not acknowledge her as Mine."

1316   October 1, 1937. "Daughter, I need sacrifice lovingly accomplished, because that alone has meaning for Me. Enormous indeed are the debts of the world which are due to Me; pure souls can pay them by their sacrifice, exercising mercy in spirit."

1317   I understand Your words, Lord, and the magnitude of the mercy that ought to shine in my soul. Jesus: "I know, My daughter, that you understand it and that you do everything within your power. But write this for the many souls who are often worried because they do not have the material means with which to carry out an act of mercy. Yet **spiritual mercy,** which requires neither permissions nor storehouses, is much more meritorious and **is within the grasp of every soul.** If a soul does not exercise mercy some way, it will not obtain My mercy on the day of judgment. Oh, if only souls knew how to gather eternal treasure for themselves, they would not be judged, for they would forestall My judgment with their mercy.

1578   "Let souls who are striving for perfection particularly adore My mercy, because the abundance of graces which I grant them flows from My mercy. I desire that these souls distinguish themselves by boundless trust in My mercy. I myself will attend to the sanctification of such souls. I will provide them with everything they will need to attain sanctity. The graces of **My mercy are drawn by means of one vessel only, and that is — trust.** The more a soul trusts, the more it will receive. **Souls that trust boundlessly are a great comfort to**

Me, because I pour all the treasures of My graces into them. I rejoice that they ask for much, because it is My desire to give much, very much."

1695   Then I heard the words, "I am glad you behaved like My true daughter. **Be always merciful as I am merciful.** Love everyone out of love for Me, even your greatest enemies, so that My mercy may be fully reflected in your heart."

1777   **"...Sooner would heaven and earth turn into nothingness than would My mercy not embrace a trusting soul."**

1784   Today, in the course of a long conversation, the Lord said to me, How very much I desire the salvation of souls! My dearest secretary, write that I want to pour out My divine life into human souls and sanctify them, if only they were willing to accept My grace. **The greatest sinners would achieve great sanctity, if only they would trust in My mercy.** The very inner depths of My being are filled to overflowing with mercy, and it is being poured out upon all I have created. My delight is to act in a human soul and to fill it with My mercy and to justify it. My kingdom on earth is My life in the human soul."

Chapter VI

THE MEANS OF MERCY

By which means are we to respond to the Lord's mercy? By the Sacraments of Eucharist and Reconciliation, and by the means given to Sister Faustina by the Lord; namely, the image of The Divine Mercy, the Feast of The Divine Mercy, the Novena before the Feast, the Chaplet of The Divine Mercy, and a remembrance of His agony at Three O'clock.

THE SACRAMENT OF THE EUCHARIST

The Sacrament of the Eucharist is key to the devotion of The Divine Mercy. The Eucharist is so central to the life of Sister Faustina that most of the pages of her *Diary* have some reference to it. She regularly experienced visions of the Lord at her daily Mass and many times at the time of Holy Communion. Her times of adoration of the Blessed Sacrament were always times of grace.

These entries from the *Diary* can help us, as priests, to grow in faith and reverence for the Eucharist.

344   December 20, 1934.

One evening as I entered my cell, I saw the Lord Jesus exposed in the monstrance under the open sky, as it seemed. **At the feet of Jesus I saw my confessor,** and behind him a great number of the highest ranking ecclesiastics, clothed in vestments the like of which I had never seen except in this vision; and behind them, groups of religious from various orders; and further still I saw enormous crowds of people, which extended far beyond my vision. **I saw the two rays coming out from the Host, as in the image,** closely united but not intermingled;

and they passed through the hands of my confessor, and then **through the hands of the clergy** and from their hands to the people, and then they returned to the Host... and at that moment I saw myself once again in the cell which I had just entered.

370   That same day, when I was in church waiting for confession, I saw **the same rays issuing from the monstrance and spreading throughout the church. This lasted all through the service. After the Benediction. [the rays shone out] to both sides and returned again to the monstrance.** Their appearance was bright and transparent like crystal.

442   Once when my confessor [Father Sopocko] was saying Mass, I saw, as usual, the Child Jesus on the altar, from the time of the Offertory. However, a moment before the Elevation, the priest vanished from my sight, and Jesus alone remained. **When the moment of the Elevation approached, Jesus took the Host and the chalice in His little hands and raised them together, looking up to heaven,** and a moment later I again saw my confessor. I asked the Child Jesus where the priest had been during the time I had not seen him. Jesus answered, "In My Heart." But I could not understand anything more of these words of Jesus.

616   On Thursday, when I went to my cell, I saw over me the Sacred Host in great brightness. Then I heard a voice that seemed to be coming from above the Host: In the Host is your power; It will defend you. After these words, the vision disappeared, but a strange power entered my soul, and a strange light as to what our love for God consists in; namely, in doing His will.

684   + Holy Hour. — Thursday. During this hour of prayer, **Jesus allowed me to enter the Cenacle,** and I was a witness to what happened there. However, I was most

deeply moved when, before the Consecration, Jesus raised His eyes to heaven and entered into a mysterious conversation with His Father. **It is only in eternity that we shall really understand that moment.** His eyes were like two flames; His face was radiant, white as snow; His whole personage full of majesty, His soul full of longing. At the moment of Consecration, love rested satiated — the sacrifice fully consummated. Now only the external ceremony of death will be carried out — external destruction; the **essence [of it] is in the Cenacle.** Never in my whole life had I understood this mystery so profoundly as during that Hour of Adoration. Oh, how ardently I desire that the whole world would come to know this unfathomable mystery!

757   November 19, [1936]. During Mass today, I saw the Lord Jesus, who said to me, "Be at peace, My daughter; I see your efforts, which are very pleasing to Me." And the Lord disappeared, and it was time for Holy Communion. After I received Holy Communion, I suddenly saw the Cenacle and in it Jesus and the Apostles. **I saw the institution of the Most Blessed Sacrament.** Jesus allowed me to penetrate His interior, and I came to know the greatness of His majesty and, at the same time, His great humbling of Himself. The extraordinary light that allowed me to see His majesty revealed to me, at the same time, what was in my own soul.

913   February 2, 1937. Today, from early morning, divine absorption penetrates my soul. During Mass, I thought I would see the little Jesus, as I often do; however, today during Holy Mass I saw the Crucified Jesus. Jesus was nailed to the cross and was in great agony. His suffering pierced me, soul and body, in a manner which was invisible, but nevertheless most painful.

914   **Oh, what awesome mysteries take place during Mass!** A great mystery is accomplished in the Holy Mass. With

what great devotion should we listen to and take part in this death of Jesus. **One day we will know what God is doing for us in each Mass,** and what sort of gift He is preparing in it for us. Only His divine love could permit that such a gift be provided for us. O Jesus, my Jesus, with what great pain is my soul pierced when I see this fountain of life gushing forth with such sweetness and power for each soul, while at the same time I see souls withering away and drying up through their own fault. O Jesus, grant that the power of mercy embrace these souls.

991   February 26, 1937. Today, I saw how the Holy Mysteries were being celebrated without liturgical vestments and in private homes, because of a passing storm; and **I saw the sun come out from the Blessed Sacrament,** and all other lights went out, or rather, they were dimmed; and all the people were looking toward this [one] light. But at the present time I do not understand the meaning of this vision.

1037   + I find myself so weak that were it not for Holy Communion I would fall continually. **One thing alone sustains me, and that is Holy Communion.** From it I draw my strength; in it is all my comfort. I fear life on days when I do not receive Holy Communion. I fear my own self. Jesus concealed in the Host is everything to me. From the tabernacle I draw strength, power, courage and light. Here, I seek consolation in time of anguish. I would not know how to give glory to God if I did not have the Eucharist in my heart.

1302   September 29, [1937]. Today, I have come to understand many of God's mysteries. I have come to know that Holy Communion remains in me until the next Holy Communion. A vivid and clearly felt presence of God continues in my soul. The awareness of this plunges me into deep recollection, without the slightest effort on my part. **My heart is a living tabernacle** in which the living Host is reserved. I have never sought God in some far-off place, but within myself. It is in the depths of my own being that I commune with my God.

1385   November 19. After Communion today, Jesus told me how much He desires to come to human hearts. "I desire to unite Myself with human souls; **My great delight is to unite Myself with souls.** Know, My daughter, that when I come to a human heart in Holy Communion, My hands are full of all kinds of graces which I want to give to the soul. But souls do not even pay any attention to Me; they leave Me to Myself and busy themselves with other things. Oh, how sad I am that souls do not recognize Love! They treat Me as a dead object."

1392   All the good that is in me is due to Holy Communion. I owe everything to it. **I feel that this holy fire has transformed me completely.** Oh, how happy I am to be a dwelling place for You, O Lord! My heart is a temple in which You dwell continually...

1407   When I was receiving Holy Communion today, I noticed in the cup a Living Host, which the priest gave to me. When I returned to my place I asked the Lord, "Why was one Host alive, since You are equally alive under each of the species?" The Lord answered me, "That is so. **I am the same under each of the species, but not every soul receives Me with the same living faith as you do,** My daughter, and therefore I cannot act in their souls as I do in yours."

1447   + Oh, how painful it is to Me that souls so seldom unite themselves to Me in Holy Communion. I wait for souls, and they are indifferent toward Me. I love them tenderly and sincerely, and they distrust Me. **I want to lavish My graces on them, and they do not want to accept them.** They treat Me as a dead object, whereas My Heart is full of love and mercy. In order that you may know at least some of My pain, imagine the most tender of mothers who has great love for her children, while those children spurn her love. Consider her pain. No one is in a position to console her. This is but a feeble image and likeness of My love."

1485   Conversation of the Merciful God
                         with a Sinful Soul.

Soul: Lord, I recognize your holiness, and I fear You.
Jesus: "My child, do you fear the God of mercy? My holiness (80) does not prevent Me from being merciful. Behold, for you I have established a throne of mercy on earth — the tabernacle — and from this throne I desire to enter into your heart. I am not surrounded by a retinue or guards. You can come to me at any moment, at any time; I want to speak to you and desire to grant you grace.

1683   Write for the benefit of religious souls that **it delights Me to come to their hearts in Holy Communion. But if there is anyone else in such a heart, I cannot bear it and quickly leave that heart,** taking with Me all the gifts and graces I have prepared for the soul. And the soul does not even notice My going. After some time, inner emptiness and dissatisfaction will come to her attention. Oh, if only she would turn to Me then, I would help her to cleanse her heart, and I would fulfill everything in her soul; but without her knowledge and consent, I cannot be the Master of her heart.

THE SACRAMENT OF RECONCILIATION: CONFESSORS AND SPIRITUAL DIRECTORS

The Lord speaks repeatedly about the use of the Sacrament of Reconciliation (also called the "Tribunal of Mercy"). Over and over again he calls Sister Faustina to openness and obedience to the confessor (Father Andrasz) and to her spiritual director (Father Sopocko).

The Lord described the Tribunal of Mercy as the place of the greatest mercy (1448). He himself is waiting for the sinner, using the priest as a screen (1602, 1725).

The words of our Lord about confessors and spiritual directors present much needed teaching on how to approach and instruct the penitent.

Priests in the Sacrament of Reconciliation

269　　Once, when I had finished a novena to the Holy Spirit for the intention of my confessor [Father Sopocko], the Lord answered, "I made him known to you even before your superiors had sent you here. As you **will act towards your confessor, so I will act toward you.** If you conceal something from him, even though it be the least of My graces, I too will hide Myself from you, and you will remain alone."

933　　Then I heard the following words in my soul: "**You will receive a greater reward for your obedience and subjection to your confessor than you will for the practices which you will be carrying out.** Know this, My daughter, and act accordingly: anything, no matter how small it be, that has the seal of obedience to My representative is pleasing to Me and great in My eyes."

975　　Today I heard these words: "**Pray for souls that they be not afraid to approach the tribunal of My mercy.** Do not grow weary of praying for sinners. You know what a burden their souls are to My Heart. Relieve My deathly sorrow; dispense My mercy."

1448　　"Write, speak of My mercy. Tell souls where they are to look for solace; that is, **in the Tribunal of Mercy** [the Sacrament of Reconciliation] **There the greatest miracles take place [and] are incessantly repeated.** To avail oneself of this miracle, it is not necessary to go on a great pilgrimage or to carry out some external ceremony; it suffices to come with faith to the feet of My representative and to reveal to him one's misery, and the miracle of Divine Mercy will be fully demonstrated. Were a soul like a decaying corpse so that from a human standpoint, there would be no [hope of] restoration and everything would already be lost, it is not so with God. The miracle of Divine Mercy restores that soul in full. Oh, how miserable are those who do not take advantage of the miracle of God's mercy! You will call out in vain, but it will be too late."

1602   Today the Lord said to me, "Daughter, when you go to confession, to this fountain of My mercy, the Blood and Water which came forth from My Heart always flows down upon your soul and ennobles it. Every time you go to confession, immerse yourself entirely in My mercy, with great trust, so that I may pour the bounty of My grace upon your soul. When you approach the confessional, know this, that I Myself am waiting there for you. I am only hidden by the priest, but I Myself act in your soul. Here the misery of the soul meets the God of mercy. Tell souls that from this fount of mercy souls draw graces solely with the vessel of trust. If their trust is great, there is no limit to My generosity. The torrents of grace inundate humble souls. The proud remain always in poverty and misery, because My grace turns away from them to humble souls."

1725   Today, the Lord has been teaching me, once again, how I am to approach the Sacrament of Penance: "My daughter, just as you prepare in My presence, so also you make your confession before Me. **The person of the priest is, for Me, only a screen.** Never analyze what sort of a priest it is that I am making use of; open your soul in confession as you would to Me, and I will fill it with My light."

Priests as Spiritual Directors

12   Very early the next day, I rode back into the city and entered the first church I saw. There I began to pray to know further the will of God. Holy Masses were being celebrated one after another. During one of them I heard the words: **"Go to that priest and tell him everything; he will tell you what to do next."** After the Mass I went to the sacristy. I told the priest all that had taken place in my soul, and I asked him to advise me where to take the veil, in which religious order.

362   +One day, during the morning meditation, I heard this voice: "**I myself am your director;** I was, I am, and I will be. And since you asked for visible help, I chose and gave you a director even before you had asked, for My work required this. Know that the faults you commit against him wound My Heart. Be especially on your guard againstself-willfulness; even the smallest thing should bear the seal of obedience.

979   Today at Benediction, I saw Jesus, and He spoke these words to me: **"Be obedient to your director** in everything; his word is My will. Be certain in the depths of your soul that it is I who am speaking through his lips, and I desire that you reveal the state of your soul to him with the same simplicity and candor as you have with Me. I say it again, My daughter: know that his word is My will for you.

1308   + Jesus, I have noticed that You seem to be less concerned with me. "Yes, My child, **I am replacing Myself with your spiritual director**. He is taking care of you according to My will. **Respect his every word as My own.** He is the veil behind which I am hiding. Your director and I are one; his words are My words."

1784   "Write, My secretary, that **I Myself am the spiritual guide of souls — and I guide them indirectly through the priest,** and lead each one to sanctity by a road known to Me alone."

THE IMAGE OF THE DIVINE MERCY

Our Lord asked that Sister Faustina have an image painted according to the pattern she saw and stated that this would be a vessel to draw mercy from the infinite ocean of his mercy. The image is of Jesus coming toward us with his right hand raised in blessing and his left hand touching his garment at the bosom in the area of the heart where two great rays of light shining forth, one red and the other pale. He is dressed in a white garment and is radiant with light. This image is an icon of Jesus as eternal High Priest, dressed in the white robes of the priest, coming with his hands raised in blessing, coming with salvation for those who await him, coming with the gifts of the life-giving water, blood and Spirit. This icon presents three scenes from scripture, simultaneously, like a triple-exposure photograph.

The obvious scene is that of Easter Sunday night when Jesus appeared in the upper room, coming through the locked doors of the cenacle, coming with the victorious blessings of peace, showing his wounds, giving to his apostles the authority which he received, breathing on them the Holy Spirit for the forgiveness of sins (see *Jn 20:19-31*).

The second scene is Calvary. From his pierced side, blood and water flow out as a fount of mercy for us — here seen as the red and pale rays, representing the waters of Baptism and the Blood of the Eucharist.

The third scene in Jesus as the eternal High Priest, dressed in the white linen of the priest, coming out of the Holy of Holies — this time not from the sanctuary made by human hands, but coming out of the Holy of Holies of Heaven,coming from the very mercy seat of the Father. He comes as the "Merciful One" with blessing in his raised hand and the name of the Lord on his lips (see *Sir 50:18-21* and *Lev 16:1-4*).

Jesus our High Priest "was offered once to take away the sins of [the] many: he will appear a second time to bring salvation to those who eagerly await Him" (*Heb 9:28*). He will come to bring the culmination of mercy to those who await him.

1   O Eternal Love, You command Your Sacred Image to
        be painted
    And reveal to us the inconceivable fount of mercy,
    You bless whoever approaches Your rays,
    And a soul all black will turn into snow.

            O sweet Jesus, it is here[2] You established the
                throne of Your mercy
            To bring joy and hope to sinful man.
            From Your open Heart, as from a pure fount,
            Flows comfort to a repentant heart and soul.

    May praise and glory for this Image
    Never cease to stream from man's soul.
    May praise of God's mercy pour from every heart,
    Now, and at every hour, and forever and ever.

47-49   + February 22, 1931
    In the evening, when I was in my cell, I saw the Lord Jesus clothed in a white garment. One hand [was] raised in the gesture of blessing, the other was touching the garment at the breast. From beneath the garment, slightly drawn aside at the breast, there were emanating two large rays, one red, the other pale. In silence I kept my gaze fixed on the Lord; my soul was struck with awe, but also with great joy. After a while, Jesus said to me, "**Paint an image according to the pattern you see, with the signature: Jesus, I trust in You.** I desire that this image be venerated, first in your chapel, and [then] throughout the world."

48   "**I promise that the soul that will venerate this image will not perish.** I also promise victory over [its]

enemies already here on earth, especially at the hour of death. I Myself will defend it as My own glory."

49   When I told this to my confessor, I received this for a reply: "That refers to your soul." He told me, "Certainly, paint God's image in your soul." When I came out of the confessional, I again heard words such as these: "My image already is in your soul. I desire that there be a Feast of Mercy. I want this image, which you will paint with a brush, to be solemnly blessed on the first Sunday after Easter; that Sunday is to be the Feast of Mercy."

87   Vilnius, October 26, 1934.
On Friday at ten minutes to six, when I and some of our wards were coming in from the garden to supper, I saw the Lord Jesus above our chapel, looking just as He did the first time I saw Him and just as He is painted in the image. **The two rays which emanated from the Heart of Jesus covered our chapel and the infirmary, and then the whole city, and spread out over the whole world.** This lasted about four minutes and disappeared. One of the girls, who was walking with me a little behind the others, also saw these rays, but she did not see Jesus, and she did not know where these rays were coming from. She was overwhelmed and told the other girls. They began to laugh at her, suggesting that she was imagining things or that perhaps it was light reflected by a passing airplane. But she persisted in her conviction, saying that never had she seen such rays before. When the others suggested that it might have been a searchlight, she replied that she knew very well what a searchlight was like, but never had she seen rays such as these.

After supper the girl approached me and told me she had been so moved by these rays that she could not keep silent, but wanted to tell everyone about them. Yet she had not seen Jesus. She kept telling me about these rays, and this put me in an awkward situation, as I could not tell her that I had seen the Lord Jesus. I prayed for her, asking the Lord to give her those graces of which she had such need. My heart rejoiced in the fact that Jesus takes the initiative to make Himself known, even though the occasion of such action on His part causes me annoyance. For Jesus, one can bear anything.

88   I asked Jesus whether the inscription could be: "Christ, King of Mercy." He answered, **I am King of Mercy**, but He did not say "Christ."

177   + Renewal of vows. From the moment I woke up in the morning, my spirit was totally submerged in God, in that ocean of love. I felt that I had been completely immersed in Him. During Holy Mass, my love for Him reached a peak of intensity. After the renewal of vows and Holy Communion, I suddenly saw the Lord Jesus, who said to me with great kindness, "My daughter, look at My merciful Heart." As I fixed my gaze on the Most Sacred Heart, **the same rays of light, as are represented in the image as blood and water, came forth from it,** and I understood how great is the Lord's mercy.

299   **+ The Mystery of the Soul**   Vilnius, 1934
When, on one occasion, my confessor told me to ask the Lord Jesus the meaning of the two rays in the image, I answered, "Very well, I will ask the Lord."

During prayer I heard these words within me: "**The two rays denote Blood and Water.** The pale ray stands for the Water which makes souls righteous. The red ray stands for the Blood which is the life of souls...

"These two rays issued forth from the very depths of My tender mercy when My agonized Heart was opened by a lance on the Cross.

"These rays shield souls from the wrath of My Father. Happy is the one who will dwell in their shelter, for the just hand of God shall not lay hold of him."

313 +Once, when I was visiting the artist [Eugene Kazimirowski] who was painting the image, and saw that it was not as beautiful as Jesus is, I felt very sad about it, but I hid this deep in my heart. When we had left the artist's house, Mother Superior [Irene] stayed in town to attend to some matters while I returned home alone. I went immediately to the chapel and wept a good deal. I said to the Lord, "Who will paint You as beautiful as You are?" Then I heard these words: "**Not in the beauty of the color, nor of the brush lies the greatness of this image, but in My grace.**"

327 …When I left the confessional and was passing before the Blessed Sacrament, I received an inner understanding about the inscription. Jesus reminded me of what He had told me the first time; namely, that these three words must be clearly in evidence: "**Jesus, I trust in You.**" [*"Jezu, Ufam Tobie."*] I understood that Jesus wanted the whole formula to be there, but He gave no direct orders to this effect as He did for these three words.

"**I am offering people a vessel with which they are to keep coming for graces to the fountain of mercy.** That vessel is this image with the signature: "Jesus, I trust in You."

441 Once, the image was being exhibited over the altar during the Corpus Christi procession [June 20, 1935]. When the priest exposed the Blessed Sacrament, and the choir began to sing, **the rays from the image pierced the Sacred Host and spread out all over the world.** Then I

heard these words: "These rays of mercy will pass through you, just as they have passed through this Host, and they will go out through all the world. At these words, profound joy invaded my soul.

657   June 19. When we went to the Jesuits' place for the procession of the Sacred Heart, during Vespers **I saw the same rays coming forth from the Sacred Host,** just as they are painted in the image. My soul was filled with great longing for God.

1796   Today, I saw the Sacred Heart of Jesus in the sky, in the midst of a great brilliance. **The rays were issuing from the Wound [in His side] and spreading out over the entire world.**

THE FEAST OF THE DIVINE MERCY

Our Lord asked Sister Faustina to pray and to work to have established a Feast of The Divine Mercy on the Sunday after Easter. This would be a day of total forgiveness of sins for those who approach the Eucharist and the Sacrament of Reconciliation. It would be an annual celebration like the Day of Atonement. All sins and punishment would be washed away in his infinite mercy. The texts of the liturgy for that Sunday are already on the forgiveness of sins. (The Gospel is of Jesus appearing in the upper room and bestowing the authority to forgive sins, and the other readings are on mercy (*Ps 118,* and *1Pt 1:3-9*).

88   …"I desire that this image be displayed in public on the first Sunday after Easter. **That Sunday is the Feast of Mercy.** Through the Word Incarnate, I make known the bottomless depth of My mercy."

280   Jesus commanded me to celebrate the Feast of God's Mercy on the first Sunday after Easter. [This I did] through interior recollection and exterior mortification, wearing the belt for three hours and praying continuously for sinners

and for mercy on the whole world. And Jesus said to me, "My eyes rest with pleasure upon this house today."

299-300 **I desire that the first Sunday after Easter be the Feast of Mercy.**
+"Ask of my faithful servant [Father Sopocko] that, on this day, he tell the whole world of My great mercy; that whoever approaches the Fount of Life on this day will be granted complete remission of sins and punishment."

+"Mankind will not have peace until it turns with trust to My mercy."

341 November 5, 1934. One morning, when it was my duty to open the gate to let out our people who deliver baked goods, I entered the little chapel to visit Jesus for a minute and to renew the intentions of the day. Today, Jesus, I offer You all my sufferings, mortifications and prayers for the intentions of the Holy Father, so that he may approve the Feast of Mercy. But, Jesus, I have one more word to say to You: I am very surprised that You bid me to talk about this Feast of Mercy, for they tell me that there is already such a feast and so why should I talk about it? And Jesus said to me, "And who knows anything about this feast? No one! Even **those who should be proclaiming My mercy and teaching people about it often do not know about it themselves.** That is why I want the image to be solemnly blessed on the first Sunday after Easter, and I want it to be venerated publicly so that every soul may know about it.

420 Sunday, [April] 28, 1935.

Low Sunday; that is, the Feast of The Divine Mercy, the conclusion of the Jubilee of Redemption. When we went to take part in the celebrations, my heart leapt with joy that the two solemnities were so closely united. I asked God for mercy on the souls of sinners. Toward the end of the service, when the priest took the Blessed Sacrament to bless the people, I saw the Lord Jesus as He is represented in the image. The Lord gave His blessing, and the rays extended over the whole world. Suddenly, I saw an impenetrable brightness in the form of a crystal dwelling place, woven together from waves of a brilliance unapproachable to both creatures and spirits. Three doors led to this resplendence. At that moment, Jesus, as He is represented in the image, entered this resplendence through the second door to the Unity within. It is a triple Unity, which is incomprehensible — which is infinity. I heard a voice, **"This Feast emerged from the very depths of My mercy, and it is confirmed in the vast depths of My tender mercies.** Every soul believing and trusting in My mercy will obtain it." I was overjoyed at the immense goodness and greatness of my God.

570   On one occasion, I saw Jesus in a bright garment; this was in the greenhouse. [He said to me,] "Write what I say to you. My delight is to be united with you. With great desire, I wait and long for the time when I shall take up My residence sacramentally in your convent.... No soul will be justified until it turns with confidence to My mercy, and this is why the first Sunday after Easter is to be the Feast of Mercy. **On that day, priests are to tell everyone about My great and unfathomable mercy.** I am making you the administrator of My mercy. Tell the confessor that the Image is to be on view in the church and not within the enclosure in that convent. By means of this Image I shall be granting many graces to souls; so, let every soul have access to it."

699   On one occasion, I heard these words: "My daughter, tell the whole world about My inconceivable mercy. **I desire that the Feast of Mercy be a refuge and shelter for all souls,** and especially for poor sinners. On that day the very depths of My tender mercy are open. I pour out a whole ocean of graces upon those souls who approach the fount of My mercy. The soul that will go to

Confession and receive Holy Communion shall obtain complete forgiveness of sins and punishment. On that day are open all the divine floodgates through which graces flow. Let no soul fear to draw near to Me, even though its sins be as scarlet. My mercy is so great that no mind, be it of man or of angel, will be able to fathom it throughout all eternity. Everything that exists has come forth from the very depths of My most tender mercy. Every soul in its relation to Me will contemplate My love and mercy throughout eternity. The Feast of Mercy emerged from My very depths of tenderness. (139) It is My desire that it be solemnly celebrated on the first Sunday after Easter. Mankind will not have peace until it turns to the Fount of My Mercy."

964   February 17, 1937, This morning during Holy Mass, I saw the Suffering Jesus. His Passion was imprinted on my body in an invisible manner, but no less painfully.

965   Jesus looked at me and said, "Souls perish in spite of My bitter Passion. **I am giving them the last hope of salvation; that is, the Feast of My Mercy.** If they will not adore My mercy, they will perish for all eternity. Secretary of My mercy, write, tell souls about this great mercy of Mine, because the awful day, the day of My justice, is near."

1109   ... He spoke these words to me: **"I want to grant a complete pardon to the souls that will go to Confession and receive Holy Communion on the Feast of My Mercy."** Then He said to me, "My daughter, fear nothing...."

1515   + I spent this whole night with Jesus in the dark dungeon. This was a night of adoration. The sisters were praying in the chapel, and I was uniting myself with them in spirit, because poor health prevents me from going to the chapel. But all night long I could not fall asleep, so I spent the night in the dark prison with Jesus. Jesus gave me to know of the sufferings He experienced there. The world will learn about them on the day of Judgment.

1516   "My daughter, tell souls that I am giving them My mercy as a defense. I Myself am fighting for them and am bearing the just anger of My Father."

1517   "Say, My daughter, that **the Feast of My Mercy has issued forth from My very depths for the consolation of the whole world.**"

THE NOVENA

In preparation for the Feast of The Divine Mercy the Lord asked for a novena of prayer from Good Friday to the following Saturday. The matter for each day's prayer was given to Sister Faustina by the Lord, and it reflects the intercessions of the Good Friday Liturgy. They are prayers for all mankind, for priests and religious, for devout souls, for those who don't know the Lord, for the separated brethren, for meek and humble souls, for souls who glorify His mercy for souls in purgatory, and for lukewarm souls.

1059   **Jesus is commanding me to make a novena before the Feast of Mercy,** and today I am to begin it for the conversion of the whole world and for the recognition of The Divine Mercy... "so that every soul will praise My goodness. I desire trust from My creatures. Encourage souls to place great trust in My fathomless mercy. Let the weak, sinful soul have no fear to approach Me, for even if it had more sins than there are grains of sand in the world, all will be drowned in the unmeasurable depths of My mercy."

1209   Novena to The Divine Mercy which Jesus instructed me to write down and make before the Feast of Mercy. It begins on Good Friday.

I desire that during these nine days you bring souls to the fountain of My mercy, that they may draw therefrom strength and refreshment and whatever grace they need in the hardships of life, and especially at the hour of death.

"On each day you will bring to My Heart a different group of souls, and you will immerse them in this ocean of My mercy, and I will bring all these souls into the house of My Father. You will do this in this life and in the next. **I will deny nothing to any soul whom you will bring to the fount of My mercy.** On each day you will beg My Father, on the strength of My bitter Passion, for graces for these souls."

I answered, "Jesus, I do not know how to make this novena or which souls to bring first into Your Most Compassionate Heart." Jesus replied that He would tell me which souls to bring each day into His Heart.

THE CHAPLET OF THE DIVINE MERCY

The Chaplet of The Divine Mercy is an intercessory prayer that extends the offering of the Eucharist. It is a priestly prayer, prayed on the rosary beads beginning with the Our Father, Hail Mary, and the Creed. The Prayer on the large beads: "Eternal Father, I offer You the body and Blood, Soul and Divinity of Your dearly beloved Son, Our Lord Jesus Christ, in atonement for our sins and those of the whole world." On the small beads: "For the sake of His sorrowful Passion have mercy on us and on the whole world." In conclusion, prayed three times: "Holy God, Holy Mighty One, Holy Immortal One, have mercy on us and on the whole world."

The words of the Chaplet reflect Council of Trent's dogmatic definition of the Real Presence in the Eucharist and the text of 1 Jn 2:2: "He is the atoning sacrifice for our sins, and not only ours but also for the sins of the whole world." One of the most ancient intercessory prayers addressed to the Most Holy Trinity — used most widely in the Byzantine Church, and only on Good Friday in the Roman Catholic Church — concludes the chaplet.

The Chaplet is an extraordinarily powerful prayer for the dying, for the conversion of sinners, and for averting natural catastrophes according to the testimony of Sister Faustina and also the testimony of many who pray it regularly.

474　　The following day, Friday, September 13, 1935.
　　　　In the evening, when I was in my cell, I saw an Angel, the executor of divine wrath. He was clothed in a dazzling robe, his face gloriously bright, a cloud beneath his feet. From the cloud, bolts of thunder and flashes of lightning were springing into his hands; and from his hand they were going forth, and only then were they striking the earth. When I saw this sign of divine wrath which was about to strike the earth, and in particular a certain place, which for good reasons I cannot name, I began to implore the Angel to hold off for a few moments, and the world would do penance. But my plea was a mere nothing in the face of the divine anger. Just then I saw the Most Holy Trinity. The greatness of Its majesty pierced me deeply, and I did not dare to repeat my entreaties. At that very moment I felt in my soul the power of Jesus' grace, which dwells in my soul. When I became conscious of this grace, I was instantly snatched up before the Throne of God. Oh, how great is our Lord and God and how incomprehensible His holiness! I will make no attempt to describe this greatness, because before long we shall all see Him as He is. **I found myself pleading with (197) God for the world with words heard interiorly.**

54

As I was praying in this manner, I saw the Angel's helplessness: he could not carry out the just punishment which was rightly due for sins. Never before had I prayed with such inner power as I did then.

475 **The words with which I entreated God are these: Eternal Father, I offer You the Body and Blood, Soul and Divinity of Your dearly beloved Son, Our Lord Jesus Christ for our sins and those of the whole world; for the sake of His sorrowful Passion, have mercy on us.**

476 The next morning, when I entered chapel, I heard these words interiorly: "Every time you enter the chapel, immediately recite the prayer which I taught you yesterday." When I had said the prayer, in my soul I heard these words: "**This prayer will serve to appease My wrath.** You will recite it for nine days, on the beads of the rosary, in thefollowing manner: First of all, you will say one OUR FATHER and HAIL MARY and the I BELIEVE IN GOD. Then on the OUR FATHER beads you will say the following words: 'Eternal Father, I offer You the Body and Blood, Soul and Divinity of Your dearly beloved Son, Our Lord Jesus Christ, in atonement for our sins and those of the whole world.' On the HAIL MARY beads you will say the following words: 'For the sake of His sorrowful Passion have mercy on us and on the whole world.' In conclusion, three times you will recite these words: 'Holy God, Holy Mighty One, Holy Immortal One, have mercy on us and on the whole world.' "

687 Once, as I was going down the hall to the kitchen, I heard these words in my soul: **Say unceasingly the chaplet that I have taught you.** Whoever will recite it will receive great mercy at the hour of death. **Priests will recommend it to sinners as their last hope of salvation.** Even if there were a sinner most hardened, if he were to recite this chaplet only once, he will receive grace from

My infinite mercy. I desire that the whole world know My infinite mercy. I desire to grant unimaginable graces to those souls who trust in My mercy.

714   + The Lord said to me today: "Go to the Superior and tell her that **I want all the sisters and wards to say the chaplet which I have taught you.** They are to say it for nine days in the chapel in order to appease My Father and to entreat God's mercy for Poland."

754   **+ The Lord's Promise:** "The souls that say this chaplet will be embraced by My mercy during their lifetime and especially at the hour of their death."

796   The Lord told me to say this chaplet for nine days before the Feast of Mercy. It is to begin on Good Friday. "By this novena, I will grant every possible grace to souls."

810   The following afternoon, when I entered the ward, I saw someone dying, and learned that the agony had started during the night. When I verified it — it had been at the time when I had been asked for prayer. And just then, I heard a voice in my soul: **"Say the chaplet which I taught you."** I ran to fetch my rosary and knelt down by the dying person and, with all the ardor of my soul, I began to say the chaplet. Suddenly the dying person opened her eyes and looked at me; I had not managed to finish the entire chaplet when she died, with extraordinary peace. I fervently asked the Lord to fulfill the promise He had given me for the recitation of the chaplet. The Lord gave me to know that the soul had been granted the grace He had promised me. That was the first soul to receive the benefit of the Lord's promise. I could feel the power of mercy envelop that soul.

811   When I entered my solitude, I heard these words: "**At the hour of their death, I defend as My own glory every soul that will say this chaplet; or when others**

say it for a dying person, the indulgence is the same. When this chaplet is said by the bedside of a dying person, God's anger is placated, unfathomable mercy envelops the soul, and the very depths of My tender mercy are moved for the sake of the sorrowful Passion of My Son."

847-8   As penance, Father told me to say the chaplet that Jesus had taught me. While I was saying the chaplet, I heard a voice which said, **"Oh, what great graces I will grant to souls who say this chaplet..."**

929   And the Lord said to me, "My daughter, those words of your heart are pleasing to Me, and **by saying the chaplet you are bringing humankind closer to Me."**

1035   + This evening, a certain young man was dying; he was suffering terribly. For his intention, I began to say the chaplet which the Lord had taught me. I said it all, but the agony continued. I wanted to start the Litany of the Saints, but suddenly I heard the words, **Say the chaplet.** I understood that the soul needed the special help of prayers and great mercy. And so I locked myself in my room and fell prostrate before God and begged for mercy upon that soul. Then I felt the great majesty of God and His great justice. I trembled with fear, but did not stop begging the Lord's mercy for that soul. Then I took the cross off my breast, the crucifix I had received when making my vows, and I put it on the chest of the dying man and said to the Lord, "Jesus, look on this soul with the same love with which You looked on my holocaust on the day of my perpetual vows, and by the power of the promise which You made to me in respect to the dying and those who would invoke Your mercy on them, [grant this man the grace of a happy death]." His suffering then ceased, and he died peacefully. Oh, how much we should pray for the dying! Let us take advantage of mercy while there is still time for mercy.

1036   + I realize more and more how much every soul needs God's mercy throughout life and particularly at the hour of death. **This chaplet mitigates God's anger, as He Himself told me.**

1128   May 22, 1937. The heat is so intense today that it is difficult to bear. We are all thirsting for rain, and still it does not come. For several days the sky has been overcast, but there is no rain. When I looked at the plants, thirsting for the rain I was moved with pity, and **I decided to say the Chaplet until the Lord would send us rain.** Before supper, the sky covered over with clouds, and a heavy rain fell on the earth. I had been saying this prayer without interruption for three hours. **And the Lord let me know that everything can be obtained by means of this prayer.**

1540   January 28, 1938. Today the Lord said to me, "My daughter, write down these words: All those souls who will glorify My mercy and spread its worship, encouraging others to trust in My mercy, will not experience terror at the hour of death. My mercy will shield them in that final battle...

1541   My daughter, encourage souls to say the chaplet which I have given to you. **It pleases Me to grant everything they ask of Me by saying the Chaplet.** When hardened sinners say it, I will fill their souls with peace, and the hour of their death will be a happy one.

     Write this for the benefit of distressed souls; when a soul sees and realizes the gravity of it sins, when the whole abyss of the misery into which it immersed itself is displayed before its eyes, let it not despair, but with trust let it throw itself into the arms of My mercy, as a child into the arms of its beloved mother. These souls have a right of priority to My compassionate Heart, they have first access to My mercy. Tell them that no soul that has called upon My mercy has been dis-appointed or brought to shame. I delight particularly in a soul which has placed its trust in My goodness.

Write that **when they say this Chaplet in the presence of the dying, I will stand between My Father and the dying person, not as the just Judge but as the merciful Savior.**

1565   When I entered the chapel for a moment, the Lord said to me, My daughter, help Me to save a certain dying sinner. Say the Chaplet that I have taught you for him. When I began to say the Chaplet, I saw the man dying in the midst of terrible torment and struggle. His Guardian Angel was defending him, but he was, as it were, powerless against the enormity of the soul's misery. A multitude of devils was waiting for the soul. But while I was saying the Chaplet, I saw Jesus just as He is depicted in the image. The rays which issued from Jesus' heart enveloped the sick man, and the powers of darkness fled in panic. The sick man peacefully breathed his last. When I came to myself, **I understood how very important the chaplet was for the dying.** It appeases the anger of God.

1791   When a great storm was approaching, I began to say the Chaplet. Suddenly I heard the voice of an angel: "I cannot approach in this storm, because the light which comes from her mouth drives back both me and the storm." Such was the angel's complaint to God. I then recognized how much havoc he was to have made through this storm; but I also recognized that **this prayer was pleasing to God, and that this Chaplet was most powerful.**

1797   Today, the Lord came to me and said, "**My daughter, help Me to save souls. You will go to a dying sinner, and you will continue to recite the chaplet, and in**

this way you will obtain for him trust in My mercy, for he is already in despair."

1798   Suddenly, I found myself in a strange cottage where an elderly man was dying amidst great torments. All about the bed was a multitude of demons and the family, who were crying. When I began to pray, the spirits of darkness fled, with hissing and threats directed at me. The soul became calm and, filled with trust, rested in the Lord.

At the same moment, I found myself again in my own room. How this happens... I do not know.

THE THREE O'CLOCK HOUR

The Lord asked Sister Faustina to pray especially for sinners at three o'clock in the afternoon, the moment of the death of the Lord on the cross. He said that this is the hour of great mercy for the world. It is a prayer break for a moment of reflection on his passion and death for us. If possible, it is a good time to make a visit to the Blessed Sacrament, and an excellent time for making the Stations of the Cross.

414   **On Good Friday, at three o'clock in the afternoon,** when I entered the chapel, I heard these words: "I desire that the image be publicly honored." Then I saw the Lord Jesus dying on the Cross amidst great suffering, and out of the Heart of Jesus came the same two rays as are in the image.

648   **Good Friday. At three o'clock,** I saw the Lord Jesus, crucified, who looked at me and said, "I thirst." Then I saw two rays issue from His side, just as they appear in the image. I then felt in my soul the desire to save souls and to empty myself for the sake of poor sinners. I offered myself, together with the dying Jesus, to the Eternal Father, for the salvation of the whole world. With Jesus, through Jesus and in Jesus is my communion with

You, Eternal Father. On Good Friday, Jesus suffered in His soul in a way which was different from [His suffering on] Holy Thursday.

1319   You expired, Jesus, but the source of life gushed forth for souls, and the ocean of mercy opened up for the whole world. O Fount of Life, unfathomable Divine Mercy, envelop the whole world and empty Yourself out upon us.

1320   **At three o'clock, implore My mercy, especially for sinners;** and, if only for a brief moment, immerse yourself in My Passion, particularly in My abandonment at the moment of agony. **This is the hour of great mercy for the whole world.** I will allow you to enter into My mortal sorrow. In this hour, I will refuse nothing to the soul that makes a request of Me in virtue of My Passion....

1572   "I remind you, My daughter, that **as often as you hear the clock strike the third hour, immerse yourself completely in My mercy, adoring and glorifying it;** invoke its omnipotence for the whole world, and particularly for poor sinners; for at that moment mercy was opened wide for every soul. In this hour you can obtain everything for yourself and for others for the asking; **it was the hour of grace for the whole world — mercy triumphed over justice.**

My daughter, try your best to make the Stations of the Cross in this hour, provided that your duties permit it; and if you are not able to make the Stations of the Cross, then at least step into the chapel for a moment and adore, in the Blessed Sacrament, My Heart, which is full of mercy; and should you be unable to step into the chapel, immerse yourself in prayer there where you happen to be, if only for a very brief instant. I claim veneration for My mercy from every creature, but above all from you, since it is to you that I have given the most profound understanding of this mystery.

Chapter VII

THE COST OF MERCY

The cost of this mercy so lavishly poured out was the passion, death, and resurrection of the Lord Jesus. To be such an effective secretary and apostle of mercy, Sister Faustina shared in the cost — she asked and agreed to suffer whatever the Lord sent her, and this, for the salvation of souls. Her Diary records the price she willingly paid for being such an open channel of God's mercy. She suffered terribly from tuberculosis, offering all for the salvation of souls. Regularly, especially on Fridays, she shared in the Passion of the Lord.

The words of Our Lord to Sister Faustina show the value of suffering in union with him for the salvation of souls. Also the words of Sister Faustina describe her prayer and suffering for priests. What suffering she accepted for priests!

The description of her suffering for souls in general is in the appendix. There are many Diary entries in which Sister Faustina describes her sufferings in union with Christ, but these are not all listed here because they do not specifically mention that she offered these for souls — although she made a daily oblation of all her sufferings for souls.

WORDS OF OUR LORD ABOUT
SUFFERING FOR OTHERS

67   When I fell sick [probably the beginning of consumption] after my first vows and when, despite the kind and solicitous care of my Superiors and the efforts of the doctor, I felt neither better nor worse, remarks began to reach my ears which inferred that I was making believe, With that, my suffering was doubled,

and this lasted for quite a long time. One day I complained to Jesus that I was being a burden to the sisters. Jesus answered me, "**You are not living for yourself but for souls, and other souls will profit from your sufferings.** Your prolonged suffering will give them the light and strength to accept My will.

235 **O Jesus, I long for the salvation of immortal souls.** It is in sacrifice that my heart will find free expression, in sacrifice which no one will suspect. I will burn and be consumed unseen in the holy flames of the love of God. The presence of God will help my sacrifice to be perfect and pure.

279 God made known to me what true love consists in and gave light to me about how, in practice, to give proof of it to Him. True love of God consists in carrying out God's will. To show God our love in what we do, all our actions, even the least, must spring from our love of God. And the Lord said to me, "**My child, you please Me most by suffering.** In your physical as well as your mental sufferings, My daughter, do not seek sympathy from creatures. I want the fragrance of your suffering to be pure and unadulterated. I want you to detach yourself, not only from creatures, but also from yourself. My daughter, I want to delight in the love of your heart, a pure love, virginal, unblemished, untarnished. **The more you will come to love suffering, My daughter, the purer your love for Me will be.**"

282 Once the Lord said to me, "**My Heart was moved by great mercy towards you, My dearest child, when I saw you torn to shreds because of the great pain you suffered in repenting for your sins.** I see your love, so pure and true that I give you first place among the virgins. You are the honor and glory of My Passion. I see every abasement of your soul, and nothing escapes my attention. **I lift up the humble even to my very throne, because I want it so.**"

323   **I united my sufferings with the sufferings of Jesus and offered them for myself and for the conversion of souls who do not trust in the goodness of God.** Suddenly, my cell was filled with black figures full of anger and hatred for me. One of them said, "Be damned, you and He who is within you, for you are beginning to torment us even in hell." As soon as I said, "And the Word was made flesh and dwelt among us," the figures vanished in a sudden whir.

943   + Today, I feel such desolation in my soul that I do not know how to explain it even to myself. I would like to hide from people and cry endlessly. **No one understands a heart wounded by love,** and when such a heart feels itself abandoned interiorly, no one can comfort it. O souls of sinners, you have taken the Lord away from me, but all right, all right; you get to know how sweet the Lord is, and let the whole sea of bitterness flood my heart. I have given all my divine comforts to you.

964-5   February 17, 1937, This morning during Holy Mass, I saw the Suffering Jesus. **His Passion was imprinted on my body in an invisible manner, but no less painfully.** Jesus looked at me and said, "Souls perish in spite of My bitter Passion. I am giving them the last hope of salvation; that is, the Feast of My Mercy...."

1032   + During Holy Mass, I saw the Lord Jesus nailed upon the Cross amidst great torments. A soft moan issued from His Heart. After some time, He said, "I thirst. I thirst for the salvation of souls. Help Me, My daughter, to save souls. **Join your sufferings to My Passion and offer them to the heavenly Father for sinners."**

1033   **+ When I see that the burden is beyond my strength, I do not consider or analyze it or probe into it, but I run like a child to the Heart of Jesus and say only one word to Him: "You can do all things."** And then I keep silent, because I know that Jesus himself will intervene in thematter, and as for me, instead of tormenting myself, I use that time to love Him.

1034   Monday of Holy Week. **I asked the Lord to let me take part in His Sorrowful Passion that I might experience in soul and body, to the extent that this is possible for a creature, His bitter Passion.** I asked to experience all the bitterness, in so far as this was possible. And the Lord answered that He would give me this grace, and that on Thursday, after Holy Communion, He would grant this in a special way.

1425   Today, for a short while, **I experienced the pain of the crown of thorns. I was praying for a certain soul before the Blessed Sacrament at the time.** In an instant, I felt such a violent pain that my head dropped onto the altar rail. Although this moment was very brief, it was very painful.

1468   For quite a long while, I felt pain in my hands, feet and side. Then I saw a certain sinner who, profiting from my sufferings, drew near to the Lord. All this for starving souls that they may not die of starvation.

1625   March 2, [1938]. I began Holy Lent in the way that Jesus wanted me to, making myself totally dependent upon His holy will and accepting with love everything that He sends me. I cannot practice any greater mortifications, because I am so very weak. This long illness has sapped my strength completely. **I am uniting myself with Jesus through suffering. When I meditate on His Painful Passion, my physical sufferings are lessened.**

1626   The Lord said to me, "I am taking you into My school for the whole of Lent. **I want to teach you how to suffer**...."

SUFFERING FOR PRIESTS

41   On one occasion I saw a servant of God in the immediate danger of committing a mortal sin. **I started to beg God to deign to send down upon me all the torments of hell and all the sufferings He wished if only this priest would be set free and snatched from the occasion of committing a sin.** Jesus heard my prayer and, that very instant, I felt a crown of thorns on my head. The thorns penetrated my head with great force right into my brain. This lasted for three hours; the servant of God was set free from this sin, and his soul was strengthened by a special grace of God.

531   November 24, 1935. Sunday, first day. I went at once before the Blessed Sacrament and offered myself with Jesus, present in the Most Holy Sacrament, to the Everlasting Father. Then I heard these words in my soul: "Your purpose and that of your companions is to unite yourselves with Me as closely as possible; through love You will reconcile earth with heaven, you will soften the just anger of God, and you will plead for mercy for the world. **I place in your care two pearls very precious to My Heart: these are the souls of priests and religious. You will pray particularly for them; their power will come from your diminishment.** You will join prayers, fasts, mortifications, labors and all sufferings to My prayer, fasting, mortification, labors and sufferings and then they will have power before My Father."

596   **Once, a certain priest [Father Sopocko] asked me to pray for him.** I promised to pray, and asked for a mortification. When I received permission for a certain mortification, I felt a great desire to give up all the graces that God's goodness would intend for me that day in favor of that priest, and **I asked the Lord Jesus**

to deign to bestow on me all the sufferings and afflictions, both exterior and spiritual, that the priest would have had to suffer during that day. God partially answered my request and, **at once, all sorts of difficulties and adversities sprang up out of nowhere,** so much so that one of the sisters remarked out loud that the Lord Jesus must have a hand in this because everyone was trying Sister Faustina. The charges made were so groundless that what some sisters put forward, others denied, while I offered all this in silence on behalf of the priest.

But that was not all; I began to experience interior sufferings. First, I was seized by depression and aversion towards the sisters, then a kind of uncertainty began to trouble me. I could not recollect myself during prayer, and various things would take hold of my mind. When, tired out, I entered the chapel, a strange pain seized my soul, and I began to weep softly. Then I heard in my soul a voice, saying, "My daughter, why are you weeping? After all, you yourself offered to undertake these sufferings. Know that what you have taken upon yourself for that soul is only a small portion. He is suffering much more. And I asked the Lord, "Why are You treating him like that?" The Lord answered me that it was for the triple crown meant for him: that of virginity, the priesthood and martyrdom. At that moment, a great joy flooded my soul at the sight of the great glory that is going to be his in heaven. Right away I said the *Te Deum*[125] for this special grace of God; namely, of learning how God treats those He intends to have close to himself. **Thus, all sufferings are nothing in comparison with what awaits us in heaven.**

647   From this, I came to understand one thing: that **I must pray much for each** of my confessors, that he might obtain the light of the Holy Spirit, for when I approach

the confessional without first praying fervently, the confessor does not understand me very well. Father encouraged me to pray fervently for these intentions, that God would give better knowledge and understanding of the things He is asking of me. "Make novena after novena, Sister, and God will not refuse the graces."

823   December 17, [1936]. **I have offered this day for priests. I have suffered more today than ever before, both interiorly and exteriorly. I did not know it was possible to suffer so much in one day.** I tried to make a Holy Hour, in the course of which my spirit had a taste of the bitterness of the Garden of Gethsemane. I am fighting alone, supported by His arm, against all the difficulties that face me like unassailable walls. But I trust in the power of His name and I fear nothing.

953   + February 15, 1937. Today my suffering increased somewhat: I not only feel greater pain all through my lungs, but also some strange pains in my intestines. **I am suffering as much as my weak nature can bear, all for immortal souls, to plead the mercy of God for poor sinners and to beg for strength for priests.** Oh, how much reverence I have for priests; and I am asking Jesus, the High Priest, to grant them many graces.

988   I was praying for a certain priest asking God to help him in certain matters when I suddenly saw Jesus Crucified. His eyes were closed, and He was immersed in torture. **I worshiped His five wounds, each one separately, and asked His blessing for him.** Jesus gave me to know interiorly how dear that soul was to Him, and I felt that grace was flowing from Jesus' wounds upon that soul who, like Jesus, is also stretched upon the Cross.

1212   **"Today bring to me the souls of priests and religious, and immerse them in My unfathomable mercy.** It was they who gave Me the strength to endure My bitter Passion. Through them, as through channels, My mercy flows out upon mankind."

1607   [February] 16, 1938. **As I was praying** to the living Heart of Jesus in the Blessed Sacrament **for the intention of a certain priest,** Jesus suddenly gave me knowledge of His goodness and said to me, I will give him nothing that is beyond his strength."

Chapter VIII

REFLECTIONS

What words of strength and consolation! Jesus wants his mercy made known. He wants his priests to proclaim it, especially to sinners. The promise of anointing the priest's words and the hearts of his listeners when he proclaims and glorifies the Lord's mercy is an exciting promise which challenges me to take advantage of it. I've consciously and regularly spoken of the Lord's mercy, and I've seen the effect it has on listeners.

Jesus wants priest to beg for his mercy especially upon those in misery. My prayer for mercy often consists of plunging a given situation or person into the infinite ocean of divine mercy. Or at other times simply crying out "Jesus Mercy!" When we turn to him, he fulfills his great desire to pour out his mercy upon souls, and so is comforted in his burning desire to love us.

On the other hand, the Lord is deeply saddened by chosen souls — especially priests and religious — who do not turn to his mercy and do not understand it.

The devotion to The Divine Mercy, in a sense, is capsulized in the beatitude: "Blessed are the merciful for they shall obtain mercy." Those who are merciful to others — by thought, word, and deed — will themselves obtain mercy, because only the merciful will obtain mercy. Jesus Himself is the first and foremost man of mercy who obtained mercy from the Father, was raised from the dead to new life, and ascended to the throne of the Father. Jesus trusted in the merciful Father and has commanded us to "Be merciful, even as your Father is merciful" (*Lk 6:36 RSV*).

The short prayer "Jesus, I Trust in You!" also capsulizes the devotion to The Divine Mercy. To trust in Him is the first and foremost response to His mercy. To trust Him we must be merciful; to be merciful we must trust Him. He alone is the source of mercy. In Him alone we place our trust.

I sense the growing urgency to proclaim the Lord's mercy. The times are so urgent because the Lord's day of judgment is approaching. There are millions upon millions of souls that are in sin and darkness and do not even know about The God of mercy.

It is the duty of each of us priests to proclaim and to beg for God's mercy for the people while there is still time in this day of mercy. Such is the urgency of this devotion to The Divine Mercy.

Appendix I

WORDS OF SISTER FAUSTINA AND/OR OUR LORD

A. ON SUFFERING FOR OTHERS

57 My desires are mad and unattainable. I wish to conceal from You that I suffer. I want never to be rewarded for my efforts and my good actions. You yourself, Jesus, are my only reward; You are enough, O Treasure of my heart! **I want to share compassionately in the sufferings of my neighbors and to conceal my own sufferings, not only from them, but also from You, Jesus.**

Suffering is a great grace; through suffering the soul becomes like the Savior; in suffering love becomes crystallized; the greater the suffering, the purer the love.

135 During the third probation, **the Lord gave me to understand that I should offer myself to Him so that He could do with me as He pleased. I was to remain standing before Him as a victim offering.** At first, I was quite frightened, as I felt myself to be so utterly miserable and knew very well that this was the case. I answered the Lord once again, "I am misery itself; how can I be a hostage [for others]?" "You do not understand this today. Tomorrow, during your adoration, I will make it known to you." My heart trembled, as did my soul, so deeply did these words sink into my soul. The word of God is living.

72

When I came to the adoration, I felt within my soul that I had entered the temple of the living God, whose majesty is great and incomprehensible. And He made known to me what even the purest spirits are in His sight. Although I saw nothing externally, God's presence pervaded me. At that very moment, my intellect was strangely illumined. A vision passed before the eyes of my soul; it was like the vision Jesus had in the Garden of Olives. First, the physical sufferings and all the circumstances that would increase them; [then] the full scope of the spiritual sufferings and those that no one would know about. Everything entered into the vision: false suspicions, loss of good name. I've summarized it here, but this knowledge was already so clear that what I went through later on was in no way different from what I had known at that moment. **My name is to be: "sacrifice."**

When the vision ended, a cold sweat bathed my forehead. Jesus made it known to me that, even if I did not give my consent to this, I could still be saved; and He would not lessen His graces, but would still continue to have the same intimate relationship with me, so that even if I did not consent to make this sacrifice, God's generosity would not lessen thereby.

136 **And the Lord gave me to know that the whole mystery depended on me, on my free consent to the sacrifice given with full use of my faculties. In this free and conscious act lies the whole power and value before His Majesty.** Even if none of these things for which I offered myself would ever happen to me, before the Lord everything was as though it had already been consummated.

At that moment, I realized I was entering into communion with the incomprehensible Majesty. I felt that God was waiting for my word, for my consent. Then my spirit immersed itself in the Lord, and I said, **"Do**

with me as You please. I subject myself to Your will.
As of today, Your holy will shall be my nourishment, and
I will be faithful to Your commands with the help of Your
grace. Do with me as You please. I beg You, O Lord, be
with me at every moment of my life."

190   Once during an Adoration, **the Lord demanded that I**
        give myself up to Him as an offering, by bearing a
        certain suffering in atonement, not only for the sins of
        the world in general, but specifically for transgres-
        sions committed in this house. Immediately I said,
        "Very good; I am ready." But Jesus gave me to see what
        I was going to suffer, and in one moment the whole pas-
        sion unfolded itself before my eyes. Firstly, my inten-
        tions will not be recognized; there will be all kinds of
        suspicion and distrust as well as various kinds of humil-
        iations and adversities. I will not mention everything
        here. All these things stood before my soul's eye like a
        dark storm from which lightning was ready to strike at
        any moment, waiting only for my consent. For a
        moment, my nature was frightened. Then suddenly the
        dinner bell rang. I left the chapel, trembling and unde-
        cided. But the sacrifice was ever present before me, for I
        had neither decided to accept it, nor had I refused the
        Lord. I wanted to place myself completely in His will. If
        the Lord Jesus Himself were to impose it on me, I was
        ready. But Jesus gave me to know that I myself
        was to give my free consent and accept it with full
        consciousness, or else it would be meaningless. Its whole
        power was contained in my free act before God. But at
        the same time, Jesus gave me to understand that the deci-
        sion was completely within my power. I could do it or
        not do it. **And so I then answered immediately, "Jesus,**
        I accept everything that You wish to send me; I trust
        in Your goodness." At that moment, I felt that by this act
        I glorified God greatly. But I armed myself with
        patience. As soon as I left the chapel, I had an encounter
        with reality. I do not want to describe the details, but

there was as much of it as I was able to bear. I would not have been able to bear even one drop more.

192   Once, I took upon myself a terrible temptation which one of our students in the house at Warsaw was going through. It was the temptation of suicide. **For seven days I suffered; and after the seven days Jesus granted her the grace which was being asked, and then my suffering also ceased.** It was a great suffering. I often take upon myself the torments of our students. Jesus permits me to do this, and so do my confessors.

194   +March 27. **I desire to struggle, toil and empty myself for our work of saving immortal souls.** It does not matter if these efforts should shorten my life; it is no longer mine, but belongs to the Community. I want to be useful to the whole Church by being faithful to my Community.

195   O Jesus, today my soul is as though darkened by suffering. Not a single ray of light. The storm is raging, and Jesus is asleep. O my Master, I will not wake You; I will not interrupt Your sweet sleep. I believe that You fortify me without my knowing it

239   **+Love, it is for love of You, O Most Holy Trinity, that I offer myself to You as an oblation of praise, as a holocaust of total self-immolation.** And through this self-immolation, I desire the exaltation of Your Name, O Lord. I cast myself as a little rosebud at Your feet, O Lord, and may the fragrance of this flower be known to You alone.

243   **I will thank the Lord Jesus for every humiliation and will pray specially for the person who has given me the chance to be humiliated.** I will immolate myself for the benefit of souls. I will not count the cost of any sacrifice, I will cast myself beneath the feet of the sisters, like a carpet on which they can not only tread, but also

wipe their feet. My place is under the feet of the sisters. I will make every effort to obtain that place unnoticed by others. It is enough that God sees this.

276 **From the moment I came to love suffering, it ceased to be a suffering for me. Suffering is the daily food of my soul.**

308 1934, Holy Thursday. Jesus said to me, "**I desire that you make an offering of yourself for sinners and especially for those souls who have lost hope in God's mercy**."

309   God and Souls. An Act of Oblation.

Before heaven and earth, before all the choirs of Angels, before the Most Holy Virgin Mary, before all the Powers of heaven, I declare to the One Triune God that today, in union with Jesus Christ, Redeemer of souls, **I make a voluntary offering of myself for the conversion of sinners,** especially for those souls who have lost hope in God's mercy. **This offering consists in my accepting, with total subjection to God's will, all the sufferings, fears and terrors with which sinners are filled.** In return, I give them all the consolations which my soul receives from my communion with God. In a word, I offer everything for them: Holy Masses, Holy Communions, penances, mortifications, prayers. I do not fear the blows, blows of divine justice, because I am united with Jesus. O my God, in this way I want to make amends to You for the souls that do not trust in Your goodness. I hope against all hope in the ocean of Your mercy. My Lord and my God, my portion — my portion forever, I do not base this act of oblation on my own strength, but on the strength that flows from the merits of Jesus Christ. **I will daily repeat this act of self-oblation by pronouncing the following prayer** which You Yourself have taught me, Jesus:

"O Blood and Water which gushed forth from the Heart of Jesus as a Fount of Mercy for us, I trust in You!" S. M. Faustina of the Blessed Sacrament Holy Thursday, during Holy Mass, March 29, 1934.

310 — "I am giving you a share in the redemption of mankind. You are solace in My dying hour."

311 **When I received permission from my confessor [Father Sopocko] to make this act of oblation, I soon learned that it was pleasing to God, because I immediately began to experience its effects.** In a moment my soul became like a stone — dried up, filled with torment, and disquiet. All sorts of blasphemies and curses kept pressing upon my ears. Distrust and despair invaded my heart. This is the condition of the poor people, which I have taken upon myself. At first, I was very much frightened by these horrible things, but during the first [opportune] confession, I was set at peace.

324 After Holy Communion, I saw the Lord Jesus just as I had seen Him during one Adoration. The Lord's gaze pierced my soul through and through, and not even the least speck of dust escaped His notice. And I said to Jesus, "Jesus, I thought You were going to take me." And Jesus answered, "My will has not yet been fully accomplished in you; you will still remain on earth, but not for long. I am well pleased with your trust, but your love should be more ardent. Pure love gives the soul strength at the very moment of dying. When I was dying on the cross, I was not thinking about Myself, but about poor sinners, and I prayed for them to My Father. **I want your last moments to be completely similar to Mine on the cross.** There is but one price at which souls are bought, and that is suffering united to My suffering on the cross. Pure love understands these words; carnal love will never understand them.

384 When I stayed for Adoration from nine to ten o'clock, four other sisters stayed, too. When I approached the altar and began to meditate on the Passion of the Lord Jesus, **a terrible pain immediately filled my soul because of the ingratitude of so many souls living in the world; but particularly painful was the ingratitude of souls especially chosen by God.** There is no notion or comparison [which can describe it]. At the sight of this blackest ungratefulness I felt as though my heart were torn open; my strength failed me completely, and I fell on my face, not attempting to hide my loud cries. Each time I thought of God's great mercy and of the ingratitude of souls, pain stabbed at my heart, and I understood how painfully it wounded the sweetest Heart of Jesus. With a burning heart, I renewed my act of self-oblation on behalf of sinners.

385 With joy and longing, I have pressed my lips to the bitterness of the cup which I receive each day at Holy Mass. It is the share which Jesus has allotted to me for each moment, and I will not relinquish it to anyone. I will comfort the most sweet Eucharistic Heart continuously and will play harmonious melodies on the strings of my heart. **Suffering is the most harmonious melody of all.** I will assiduously search out that which will make Your Heart rejoice today!

419 **...O Jesus, I would like to toil and wear myself out and suffer all my life for that one moment in which I saw Your glory, O Lord, and profit for souls.**

482 O my God, I am conscious of my mission in the Holy Church. It is my constant endeavor to plead for mercy for the world. I unite myself closely with Jesus and stand before Him as an atoning sacrifice on behalf of the world. God will refuse me nothing when I entreat Him with the voice of His Son. **My sacrifice is nothing in itself, but when I join it to the sacrifice of Jesus**

Christ, it becomes all-powerful and has the power to appease divine wrath. God loves us in His Son; the painful Passion of the Son of God constantly turns aside the wrath of God.

483 ...Make of me, Jesus, a pure and agreeable offering before the Face of Your Father. Jesus, transform me, miserable and sinful as I am, into Your own self (for You can do all things), and give me to Your Eternal Father. **I want to become a sacrificial host before You, but an ordinary wafer to people.** I want the fragrance of my sacrifice to be known to You alone. O Eternal God, an unquenchable fire of supplication for Your mercy burns within me. I know and understand that this is my task, here and in eternity. You Yourself have told me to speak about this great mercy and about Your goodness.

485 I accept joy or suffering, praise or humiliation with the same disposition. I remember that one and the other are passing. What does it matter to me what people say about me? I have long ago given up everything that concerns my person. **My name is host — or sacrifice,** not in words but in deeds, in the emptying of myself and in becoming like You on the Cross, O Good Jesus, my Master!

487 In the sufferings of soul or body, I try to keep silence, for then my spirit gains the strength that flows from the Passion of Jesus. **I have ever before my eyes His sorrowful Face, abused and disfigured, His divine Heart pierced by our sins and especially by the ingratitude of chosen souls.**

488 Twice I was exhorted to make myself ready for sufferings awaiting me in Warsaw. The first warning was given interiorly by a voice I heard, and the second took place during Holy Mass. Before the Elevation, I saw the Lord Jesus on the Cross and He said to me, "**Prepare**

yourself for sufferings." I thanked the Lord for the grace of this warning and said to Him, **"I am certainly not going to suffer more than You, my Savior."** However, I took this to heart and kept strengthening myself through prayer and little sufferings so that I would be able to endure it when the greater ones come.

604   At the same time, I saw a certain person [Father Sopocko] and, in part, the condition of his soul and the ordeals God was sending him. His sufferings were of the mind and in a form so acute that I pitied him and said to the Lord, "Why do you treat him like that?" And the Lord answered, "For the sake of his triple crown." And the Lord also gave me to understand what unimaginable glory awaits the person who resembles the suffering Jesus here on earth. That person will resemble Jesus in His glory. The Heavenly Father will recognize and glorify our soul to the extent that He sees in us a resemblance to His Son. I understood that this assimilation into Jesus is granted to us while we are here on earth. **I see pure and innocent souls upon whom God has exercised His justice; these souls are the victims who sustain the world and who fill up what is lacking in the Passion of Jesus.** They are not many in number. I rejoice greatly that God has allowed me to know such souls.

605   O Holy Trinity, Eternal God, I thank You for allowing me to know the greatness and the various degrees of glory to which souls attain. Oh, what a great difference of depth in the knowledge of God there is between one degree and another! Oh, if people could only know this! O my God, if I were thereby able to attain one more degree, I would gladly suffer all the torments of the martyrs put together. **Truly, all those torments seem as nothing to me compared with the**

glory that is awaiting us for all eternity. O Lord, immerse my soul in the ocean of Your divinity and grant me the grace of knowing You; for the better I know You, the more I desire You, and the more my love for You grows. I feel in my soul an unfathomable abyss which only God can fill. I lose myself in Him as a drop does in the ocean. The Lord has inclined himself to my misery like a ray of the sun upon a barren and rocky desert. And yet, under the influence of His rays, my soul has become covered with verdure, flowers, and fruit, and has become a beautiful garden for His repose.

705   September 25. I suffer great pain in my hands, feet and side, the places where Jesus' body was pierced. **I experience these pains particularly when I meet with a soul who is not in the state of grace.** Then I pray fervently that the mercy of God will embrace that soul.

871   + My Master, cause my heart never to expect help from anyone, but I will always strive to bring assistance, consolation and all manner of relief to others. **My heart is always open to the sufferings of others;** and I will not close my heart to the sufferings of others, even though because of this I have been scornfully nicknamed "dump"; that is, [because] everyone dumps his pain into my heart. [To this] I answered that everyone has a place in my heart and I, in return, have a place in the Heart of Jesus. Taunts regarding the law of love will not narrow my heart. My soul is always sensitive on this point, and Jesus alone is the motive for my love of neighbor.

926   February 9, [1937]. Shrove Tuesday. During the last two days of the carnival, I experienced the overwhelming flood of chastisements and sins. In one instant the Lord gave me a knowledge of the sins committed throughout the whole world during these days. I fainted from fright, and even though I know the depth of God's mercy, I was surprised

that God allows humanity to exist. **And the Lord gave me to know who it is that upholds the existence of mankind: it is the chosen souls. When the number of the chosen ones is complete, the world will cease to exist.**

927   On these two days, I received Holy Communion as an act of reparation, and I said to the Lord, **"Jesus, I offer everything today for sinners. Let the blows of Your justice fall on me, and the sea of Your mercy engulf the poor sinners."** And the Lord heard my prayer: many souls returned to the Lord, but I was in agony under the yoke of God's justice. I felt I was the object of the anger of the Most High God. By evening my sufferings had reached such a stage of interior desolation that moans welled up involuntarily from my breast. I locked the door of my room and began an Adoration; that is to say, a Holy Hour. Interior desolation and an experience of God's justice — that was my prayer; and the moans and pain that welled up from my soul took the place of a sweet conversation with the Lord.

963   **+ Oh, if only the suffering soul knew how it is loved by God, it would die of joy and excess of happiness!** Some day, we will know the value of suffering, but then we will no longer be able to suffer. The present moment is ours.

981   I understood that these two years of interior suffering which I have undergone in submission to God's will in order to know it better have advanced me further in perfection than the previous ten years. **For two years now, I have been on the Cross between heaven and earth.** That is to say, I am bound by the vow of obedience and must obey the superior as God Himself. And on the other hand, God makes His will known to me directly,

and so my inner torture is so great that no one will either understand or imagine these spiritual sufferings. It seems to me that it would be easier to give up my life than to go again and again through one hour of such pain. I am not even going to write much about this matter, because one cannot describe what it is like to know God's will directly and at the same time to be perfectly obedient to the divine will as expressed indirectly through the superiors. Thanks be to God that He has given me a director; otherwise, I would not have advanced one single step.

1010   + March 5, 1937. Today, I experienced the Passion of the Lord Jesus in my own body for a long while. **The pain is very great, but all this is for the sake of immortal souls.**

1016   March 15, 1937. Today, I entered into the bitterness of the Passion of the Lord Jesus. I suffered in a purely spiritual way. I learned how horrible sin was. God gave me to know the whole hideousness of sin. **I learned in the depths of my soul how horrible sin was, even the smallest sin, and how much it tormented the soul of Jesus.** I would rather suffer a thousand hells than commit even the smallest venial sin.

1022   **+ Although outwardly I meet with many sufferings and various adversities, this does not, however, lessen my interior life for a moment nor disturb my inner silence.** I do not fear at all being abandoned by creatures because, even if all abandoned me, I would not be alone, for the Lord is with me. And even if the Lord were to hide, love will know how to find Him. For love knows no gates or guards; even the keen-eyed Cherub himself, with his flaming sword, will not stop love; it will work its way through wilderness and scorching heat, through storm, thunder and darkness, and will reach the source from which it came, and there it will endure forever. All things will come to an end; but love, never.

1062   + I made an hour of adoration in thanksgiving for the graces which had been granted me and for my illness. Illness also is a great grace. I have been ill for four months, but I do not recall having wasted so much as a minute of it. **All has been for God and souls; I want to be faithful to Him everywhere.**

1263   Up to now, I have been wondering, with some fear, where these inspirations would lead me. My fear increased when the Lord made known to me that I was to leave this Congregation. This is the third year passing by since that time, and my soul has felt, in turns, enthusiasm and an urge to act — and then I have a lot of courage and strength — and then again, when the decisive moment to undertake the work draws near, I feel deserted by God, and because of this an extraordinary fear pervades my soul, and I see that it is not the hour intended by God to initiate the work. **These are sufferings about which I don't even know how to write.** God alone knows what I put up with, day and night. It seems to me that the worst torments of the martyrs would be easier for me to bear than what I am going through, though without the shedding of a drop of blood. But all this is for souls, for souls, Lord....

1264   **Act of total abandonment to the will of God, which is for me, love and mercy itself.**

Act of Oblation

Jesus-Host, whom I have this very moment received into my heart, through this union with You **I offer myself to the heavenly Father as a sacrificial host, abandoning myself totally and completely to the most merciful and holy will of my God. From today onward, Your will, Lord, is my food.** Take my whole being; dispose of me as You please. Whatever Your fatherly hand gives me, I will accept with submission, peace and joy. I fear nothing, no matter in what direction You lead me; helped by Your grace I will carry out everything You demand of me. I no longer fear any of Your inspirations nor do I probe anxiously to see where they will lead me. Lead me, O God, along whatever roads You please; I have placed all my trust in Your will which is, for me, love and mercy itself.

Bid me to stay in this convent, I will stay; bid me to undertake the work, I will undertake it; leave me in uncertainty about the work until I die, be blessed; give me death when, humanly speaking, my life seems particularly necessary, be blessed. Should You take me in my youth, be blessed; should You let me live to a ripe old age, be blessed. Should You give me health and strength, be blessed; should You confine me to a bed of pain for my whole life, be blessed. Should you give only failures and disappointments in life, be blessed. Should You allow my purest intentions to be condemned, be blessed. Should You enlighten my mind, be blessed. Should You leave me in darkness and all kinds of torments, be blessed.

From this moment on, I live in the deepest peace, because the Lord Himself is carrying me in the hollow of His hand. He, Lord of unfathomable mercy, knows that I desire Him alone in all things, always and everywhere.

1574   O my Jesus, may the last days of my exile be spent totally according to Your most holy will. I unite my sufferings, my bitterness and my last agony itself to Your Sacred Passion; and **I offer myself for the whole world to implore an abundance of God's mercy for souls,** and in particular for the souls who are in our homes. I firmly trust in Your holy will, which is mercy itself, and I rely on it totally. Your mercy will be everything for me at the last hour, as You Yourself have promised me...

1620   **+ Jesus-Host, if You Yourself did not sustain me, I would not be able to persevere on the cross.** I would not be able to endure so much suffering. But the power of Your grace maintains me on a higher level and makes my sufferings meritorious. You give me strength always to move forward and to gain heaven by force and to have love in my heart for those from whom I suffer adversities and contempt. With Your grace one can do all things.

1680   Low Sunday. Today, I again offered myself to the Lord as a holocaust for sinners. My Jesus, if the end of my life is already approaching, **I beg You most humbly, accept my death in union with You as a holocaust which I offer You today,** while I still have full possession of my faculties and a fully conscious will, and this for a three-fold purpose:

Firstly: t**hat the work of Your mercy may spread** throughout the whole world and that the Feast of The Divine Mercy may be solemnly promulgated and celebrated.

Secondly: **that sinners,** especially dying sinners, **may have recourse to Your mercy** and experience the unspeakable effects of this mercy.

Thirdly: **that all the work of Your mercy may be realized** according to Your wishes, and for a certain person who is in charge of this work...

Accept, most merciful Jesus, this, my inadequate sacrifice, which I offer to You today before heaven and earth. May Your Most Sacred Heart, so full of mercy, complete what is lacking in my offering, and offer it to Your Father for the conversion of sinners. I thirst after souls, O Christ.

B. TO CONFESSORS AND SPIRITUAL DIRECTORS

34   When I told this and certain other things to my confessor, he replied that these might really be coming from God, but that they might also be an illusion. Because of my frequent changes [of assignments], **I did not have a permanent confessor** and besides, I had great difficulty in speaking of these things. **I prayed ardently that the Lord would give me that great grace—that is, a spiritual director.** But my prayer was answered only after my perpetual vows, when I went to Vilnius. The priest was Father Sopocko. God had allowed me to see him in an interior vision even before I came to Vilnius.

35   **Oh, if only I had had a spiritual director from the beginning, then I would not have wasted so many of God's graces. A confessor can help a soul a great deal, but he can also cause it a lot of harm. Oh, how careful confessors should be about the work of God's grace in their penitents' souls! This is a matter of great importance.** By the graces given to a soul, one can recognize the degree of its intimacy with God.

75   **...When, during confession, I sense uncertainty on the part of the priest, I do not open my soul to its depths, but only accuse myself of my sins. A priest who is not at peace with himself will not be able to inspire peace in another soul.**
       O priests, you bright candles enlightening human souls, let your brightness never be dimmed. I understood that at that time it was not God's will that I uncover my soul completely. Later on, God did give me this grace.

95   ...I should add here, however, that **the soul will respond more faithfully to divine grace if it has a well-informed confessor** to whom it can confide everything.

99   …The Directress of Novices, alarmed by my appearance, sent me off to confession, but the confessor did not understand me, and I experienced no relief whatsoever. **O Jesus, give us experienced priests!**

When I told this priest I was undergoing internal tortures, he answered that he was not worried about my soul, because he saw in it a great grace of God. But I understood nothing of this, and not even the least glimmer of light broke through to my soul.

108   During those times, **I had no spiritual director;** I was without any kind of guidance whatever. I begged the Lord, but He did not give me a director. Jesus Himself has been my Master from the days of my infancy up to the present moment. He accompanied me across all the deserts and through all dangers. I see clearly that God alone could have led me through such great perils unharmed, with my soul untarnished and passing victoriously through all difficulties, immense though they were. **…Later on, the Lord did give me a director.**

112   + A few words about confession and confessors. I shall speak only of what I have experienced and gone through within my own soul. There are **three things which hinder the soul from drawing profit from confession** in these exceptional moments.

The first thing: **The confessor has little knowledge of extraordinary ways and shows surprise** if a soul discloses to him the great mysteries worked in it by God. Such surprise frightens a sensitive soul, and it notices that the confessor hesitates to give his opinion; and if it does notice this, it will not be set at peace, but will have even more doubts after confession than before, because it will sense that the confessor is trying to set it at peace while he himself is uncertain. Or else, as has happened to me, a confessor, unable to penetrate some of the soul's mysteries, refuses to hear the confession, showing a certain fear when the soul approaches the confessional.

How can a soul in this state obtain peace in the confessional when it has become so oversensitive to every word of the priest? In my opinion, at times of such special trials sent by God to a soul, the priest, if he does not understand the soul, should direct it to some other experienced and well-instructed confessor. Or else he himself should seek light in order to give the soul what it needs, instead of downrightly denying it confession. For in this way he is exposing the soul to a great danger; and more than one soul may well leave the road along which God wanted it to journey. This is a matter of great importance, for I have experienced it myself. I myself began to waver; despite special gifts from God, and even though God Himself reassured me, I have nevertheless always wanted to have the Church's seal as well.

The second thing: **The confessor does not allow the soul to express itself frankly, and shows impatience.** The soul then falls silent and does not say everything [it has to say] and, by this, profits nothing. It profits even less when the confessor, without really knowing the soul, proceeds to put it to the test. Instead of helping the soul, he does it harm. The soul is aware that the confessor does not know it, because he did not allow it to lay itself open fully as regards both its graces and its misery. And so the test is ill-adapted. I have been submitted to some tests at which I have had to laugh.

I will express this better thus: The confessor is the doctor of the soul, but how can a doctor prescribe a suitable remedy if he does not know the nature of the sickness? Never will he be able to do so. For either the remedy will not produce the desired effect, or else it will be too strong and will aggravate the illness, and some-times — God forbid — even bring about death.

I am speaking from my own experience because, in certain instances, it was the Lord himself who directly sustained me.

The third thing: **It also happens sometimes that the confessor makes light of little things.** There is nothing little in the spiritual life. Sometimes a seemingly insignificant thing will disclose a matter of great consequence and will be for the confessor a beam of light which helps him to get to know the soul. Many spiritual undertones are concealed in little things.

A magnificent building will never rise if we reject the insignificant bricks. God demands great purity of certain souls, and so He gives them a deeper knowledge of their own misery. Illuminated by light from on high, the soul can better know what pleases God and what does not. Sin depends upon the degree of knowledge and light that exists within the soul. The same is true of imperfections. Although the soul knows that it is only sin in the strict sense of the term which pertains to the sacrament of penance, yet these petty things are of great importance to a soul which is tending to sanctity, and the confessor must not treat them lightly. The patience and kindness of the confessor open the way to the innermost secrets of the soul. The soul, unconsciously as it were, reveals its abysmal depth and feels stronger and more resistant; it fights with greater courage and tries to do things better because it knows it must give an account of them.

I will mention one more thing regarding the confessor. **It is his duty to occasionally put to the test,** to try, to exercise, to learn whether he is dealing with straw, with iron or with pure gold. Each of these three types of souls needs different kinds of training. The confessor must — and this is absolutely necessary — form a clear judgment of each soul in order to know how heavy a burden it can carry at certain times, in certain circumstances, or in particular situations. As for myself, it was only later on, after many [negative] experiences, that, when I saw that I was not understood, I no longer laid bare my soul or allowed my peace to be disturbed. But this happened only when all these graces have already been submitted to the judgement of a wise, well-instructed and experienced confessor. Now I know what to go by in certain cases.

121   + There is a series of graces which God pours into the soul after these trials by fire. The soul enjoys intimate union with God. It has many visions, both corporeal and intellectual. It hears many super-natural words, and sometimes distinct orders. But despite these graces, it is not self-sufficient. In fact, it is even less so as a result of God's graces, because it is now open to many dangers and can easily fall prey to illusions. **It ought to ask God for a spiritual director; but not only must it pray for one, it must also make every effort to find a leader who is an expert in these things,** just as a military leader must know the ways along which he will lead [his followers] into battle. A soul that is united with God must be prepared for great and hard-fought battles.

+ After these purifications and tears, God abides in the soul in a special way, but the soul does not always cooperate with these graces. Not that the soul itself is not willing to work, but it encounters so many interior and exterior difficulties that it really takes a miracle to sustain the soul on these summits. **In this, it absolutely needs a director.** People have often sown doubt in my soul, and I myself have sometimes become frightened at the thought that I was, after all, an ignorant person and did not have knowledge of many things, above all, spiritual things. But when my doubts increased, I sought light from my confessor or my superiors. Yet I did not obtain what I desired.

122   When I opened myself up to my superiors, one of them
        understood my soul and the road God intended for me.
        When I followed her advice, I made quick progress
        towards perfection. But this did not last long. When I
        opened up my soul still more deeply, I did not obtain
        what I desired; it seemed to my superior that these graces
        [of which I was the object] were unlikely, and so I could
        not draw any further help from her. She told me it was
        impossible that God should commune with His creatures
        in such a way: "I fear for you, Sister; isn't this an illusion
        of some sort! You'd better go and seek the advice of a
        priest." **But the confessor did not understand me** and
        said, "You'd better go, Sister, and talk about these mat-
        ters with your superiors." And so I would go from the
        superiors to the confessor and from the confessor to the
        superiors, and I found no peace. These divine graces
        became a great suffering for me. And more than once I
        said to the Lord directly, "Jesus, I am afraid of You;
        could You not be some kind of a ghost?" Jesus always
        reassured me, but I still continued to be incredulous. It is
        a strange thing however: the more I became incredulous,
        the more Jesus gave me proofs that these things came
        from Him.

132   I must again mention that there are **some confessors
        who seem to be true spiritual fathers, but only as long
        as things go well.** When the soul finds itself in greater
        need, they become perplexed, and either cannot or will
        not understand the soul. They try to get rid of the person
        as soon as possible. But if the soul is humble, it will
        always profit in some little way or other. God Himself
        will sometimes cast a shaft of light into the depths of the
        soul, because of its humility and faith. **The confessor
        will sometimes say something he had never intended
        to say, without even realizing it himself.** Oh, let the
        soul believe that such words are the words of the Lord
        Himself! Though indeed we ought to believe that every
        word spoken in the confessional is God's, what I have

referred to above is something that comes directly from
God. And the soul perceives that the priest is not master
of himself, that he is saying things that he would rather
not say. This is how God rewards faith.

I have experienced this many times myself. A certain
very learned and respected priest, to whom I sometimes
happened to go to confession, was always severe and
opposed to these matters [which I brought up to him].
But on one occasion he replied to me, "Bear in mind,
Sister, that if God is asking this of you, you should not
oppose Him. God sometimes wants to be praised in just
this way. Be at peace; what God has started, He will finish. But I say this to you: faithfulness to God and humility. And once again: humility. Bear well in mind what I
have told you today." I was delighted, and I thought that
perhaps this priest had understood me. But it so turned
out that I never went to confession to him again.

139   Still, a soul which is faithful to God cannot confirm its
own inspirations; it **must submit them to the control of
a very wise and learned priest;** and until it is quite certain, it should remain distrustful. It should not, on its own
initiative alone, put its trust in these inspirations and all
other higher graces, because it can thus expose itself to
great losses.

Even though a soul may immediately distinguish
between false inspirations and those of God, it should
nevertheless be careful, because many things are
uncertain. God is pleased and rejoices when a soul dis-
trusts Him for His own sake; because it loves Him, it is
prudent and itself asks and searches for help to make certain that it is really God who is acting within it. And **once
a well-instructed confessor has confirmed this, the
soul should be at peace** and give itself up to God,
according to His directions; that is, according to the
directions of the confessor.

595   …Distrust hurts His most sweet Heart, which is full of goodness and incomprehensible love for us. **A priest should sometimes be distrustful in order to better ascertain the genuineness of gifts bestowed on a given soul;** and when he does so in order to direct the soul to deeper union with God, his will be a great and incomprehensible reward indeed. But there is a great difference between this and disrespect and distrust of divine graces in a soul simply because one cannot comprehend and penetrate these things with one's mind, and this latter is displeasing to the Lord. I greatly pity souls who encounter inexperienced priests.

721   **It is a great, an immeasurably great grace of God to have a spiritual director.** I feel now that, without him, I would not be able to journey alone in my spiritual life. **Great is the power of a priest.** I thank God unceasingly for giving me a spiritual director.

937   + I will say a word more about my spiritual director **It is strange that there are so few priests who know how to pour power, strength and courage into a soul so that it can make constant progress without getting tired.** Under such direction a soul, even of lesser strength, can do much for the glory of God. And **here I discovered a secret;** namely, that the confessor, or rather the **spiritual director, does not make light of the trifles that the soul brings to him.** And when the soul notices that it is being controlled in this, it begins to exert itself and does not omit the slightest opportunity to practice virtue and also avoids the smallest faults. And from these efforts, as with little stones, there rises within the soul a most beautiful temple. On the contrary, if the soul notices that the confessor neglects these little things, it likewise neglects them and ceases to give an account of them to the confessor and, worse still, will begin to grow negligent in little things. Thus, instead of going forward,

94

it gradually retreats backward and becomes aware of the situation only when it has already fallen into some serious trouble. Here, a serious question poses itself: who is at fault, the soul in question or the confessor; that is to say, the director? **It seems to me that all the blame should be put on the imprudent director;** the soul's only fault is to have taken upon itself the choice of a director. **The director could well have led the soul along the road of God's will to sanctity.**

938 The soul should have prayed ardently and at greater length for a director and should have asked the Lord himself to choose a spiritual director for it. What begins in God will be godly, and what begins in a purely human manner will remain human. God is so merciful that, in order to help a soul He Himself chooses the spiritual guide and will enlighten the soul concerning the one before whom it should uncover the most hidden depths of its soul just as it sees itself before the Lord Jesus Himself. And when the soul considers and recognizes that God has been arranging all this, it should pray fervently for the confessor that he might have the divine light to know it well. And let it not change such a director except for a serious reason. Just as it had prayed fervently and at great length in order to learn God's will before choosing a director, so too should it pray fervently and at great length to discern whether it is truly God's will that he leave this director and choose another. If God's will is not absolutely clear, he should not make this change, for a person will not go far by himself, and Satan wants just this: to have the person who is aspiring for sanctity direct himself because then, without doubt, he will never attain it.

939 There is an exception [to this], and that is when God Himself directs the person, but the director will immediately recognize that the person in question is being guided by God Himself. God will allow him to

know this clearly and distinctly, and such a person should be even more under the director's control than anyone else. In this case, the director does not so much guide and point out the road along which the soul is to journey; but rather, **he judges and confirms that the soul is following the right path and is being led by a good spirit.**

In this situation, the director should be not only holy, but also experienced and prudent, and the soul should give priority to his opinion over that of God Himself, for then the soul will be safe from illusions and deviations. A soul that will not fully submit its inspirations to the strict control of the Church; that is, to the director, clearly shows by this that a bad spirit is guiding it. The director should be extremely prudent in such cases and test the soul's obedience. **Satan can even clothe himself in a cloak of humility, but he does not know how to wear the cloak of obedience** and thus his evil designs will be disclosed. But the director should not be overly afraid of such a soul, because if God puts that special soul in his care, He will also give him great divine light regarding it, for otherwise how could he deal wisely with the great mysteries which take place between the soul and God.

940   I myself suffered a great deal and was much tried in this respect. Therefore, I am writing only about what I myself have experienced. It was only after many novenas, prayers and penances that God sent me a priest who understood my soul. **Oh, there would be many more saintly souls if there were more experienced and saintly confessors.** Many a soul, earnestly striving for sanctity, cannot manage by itself during times of trial and abandons the road to perfection.

941   O Jesus, give us fervent and holy priests! **Oh, how great is the dignity of the priest, but at the same time, how**

great is his responsibility! Much has been given you, O
priest, but much will also be demanded of you....

C. ABOUT PRIESTS

302 +O Eternal Love, I want all the souls You have created to
come to know You. **I would like to be a priest, for then
I would speak without cease about Your mercy to sinful
souls drowned in despair. I would like to be a missionary and carry the light of faith to savage nations in
order to make You known to souls,** and to be completely
consumed for them and to die a martyr's death, just as You
died for them and for me. O Jesus, I know only too well
that **I can be a priest, a missionary, a preacher, and that
I can die a martyr's death by completely emptying
myself and denying myself for love of You, O Jesus, and
of immortal souls.**

446 **Among the crucified souls, the most numerous were
those of the clergy.** I also saw some crucified souls whom
I knew, and this gave me great joy. Then Jesus said to me,
"In your meditation tomorrow, you shall think about what
you have seen today." And immediately Jesus disappeared
on me.

491 ...I desire to go throughout the whole world and speak to
souls about the great mercy of God. **Priests, help me in
this; use the strongest words [at your disposal] to
proclaim His mercy,** for every word falls short of how
merciful He really is.

578 On one occasion, **Jesus told me, concerning a certain
priest, that these present years would be the adornment
of his priestly life.** The days of suffering always seem
longer, but they too will pass, though they pass so slowly
that it seems they are moving backwards. However, their
end is near, and then will come endless and inconceivable

joy. Eternity! Who can understand this one word which comes from You, O incomprehensible God, this one word: eternity!

806   + That same day, I saw a certain priest who was surrounded by the light which flowed from Her; evidently, this soul loves the Immaculate One.

838   **+ I marvel at how many humiliations and sufferings that priest accepts in this whole matter.** I see this at particular times, and I support him with my unworthy prayers. Only God can give one such courage; otherwise one would give up. But I see with joy that all these adversities contribute to God's greater glory. **The Lord has few such souls.** O infinite eternity, you will make manifest the efforts of heroic souls, because the earth rewards their efforts with hatred and ingratitude. Such souls do not have friends; they are solitary. And in this solitude, they gain strength; they draw their strength from God alone. With humility, but also with courage, they stand firmly in the face of all the storms that beat upon them. **Like high-towering oaks, they are unmoved. And in this there is just this one secret: that it's from God that they draw this strength, and everything whatsoever they have need of, they have for themselves and for others.** They not only carry their own burden, but also know how to take on, and are capable of taking on, the burdens of others. They are pillars of light along God's ways; they live in light themselves and shed light upon others. They themselves live on the heights, and know how to show the way to lesser ones and help them attain those heights.

931   February 10, [1937]. Today is Ash Wednesday.
       During Holy Mass, I felt for a short time the Passion of Jesus in my members. **Lent is a very special time for the work of priests. We should assist them in rescuing souls.**

98

1052   O my Jesus, I beg You on behalf of the whole Church:
         Grant it love and the light of Your Spirit,
         and **give power to the words of priests** so that
         hardened hearts might be brought to repentance
         and return to You, O Lord. Lord, **give us holy priests;** You
         yourself maintain them in holiness. O Divine and Great
         High Priest, may the power of Your mercy accompany
         them everywhere and **protect them from the devil's traps
         and snares which are continually being set for the souls
         of priests.** May the power of Your mercy, O Lord, shatter
         and bring to naught all that might tarnish the sanctity of
         priests, for You can do all things.

1240   **The Lord Jesus greatly protects His representatives on
         earth.** How closely He is united with them; and He orders
         me to give priority to their opinion over His. I have come
         to know the great intimacy which exists between Jesus and
         the priest. Jesus defends whatever the priest says, and often
         complies with his wishes, and sometimes makes His own
         relationship with a soul depend on the priest's advice. O
         Jesus, through a special grace, I have come to know very
         clearly to what extent You have shared Your power and
         mystery with them, more so than with the Angels. I rejoice
         in this, for it is all for my good.

1384   I **see a certain priest whom God loves greatly, but
         whom Satan hates terribly** because he is leading
         many souls to a high degree of sanctity and has regard
         only for God's glory. But I keep asking God that
         his patience with those who constantly oppose him
         might not run out. Where Satan himself can do no harm,
         he uses people.

1455   Also on this day **I felt the prayer of a beautiful soul
         who was praying for me and giving me, in spirit, his
         priestly blessing.** I answered in return with my own
         ardent prayer.

1534   **+ I saw a certain priest's efforts in prayer.** His prayer is similar to that of the Lord Jesus in the Garden of Olives. **Oh, if that priest only knew how pleasing to God that prayer was!**

1719   + During Holy Mass, **I came to know that a certain priest does not effect much in souls because he thinks about himself and so is alone.** God's grace takes flight; he relies on trifling external things, which have no importance in the eyes of God; and, being proud, he fritters away his time, wearing himself out to no purpose.

D. ABOUT HER CONFESSOR FATHER ANDRASZ AND HER SPIRITUAL DIRECTOR FATHER SOPOCKO:

86   +[Once] **when I saw how much my confessor was to suffer because of this work** which God was going to carry out through him, fear seized me for the moment, and I said to the Lord, "Jesus, this is Your affair, so why are You acting this way toward him? It seems to me that You are making difficulties for him while at the same time ordering him to act."

     Write, that by day and by night, My gaze is fixed upon him and I permit these adversities in order to increase his merit. **I do not reward for good results but for the patience and hardship undergone for My sake.**

90   One day, **I saw interiorly how much my confessor would have to suffer:** friends will desert you while everyone will rise up against you and your physical strength will diminish. I saw you as a bunch of grapes chosen by the Lord and thrown into the press of suffering. Your soul, Father, will at times be filled with doubts about this work and about me.

I saw that God himself seemed to be opposing [him], and I asked the Lord why He was acting in this way toward him, as though He were placing obstacles in the way of his doing what He himself had asked him to do. And the Lord said, **"I am acting thus with him to give testimony that this work is Mine. Tell him not to fear anything; My gaze is on him day and night.** There will be as many crowns to form his crown as there will be souls saved by this work. It is not for the success of a work, but for the suffering that I give reward."

141   + But my torments are coming to an end. **The Lord is giving me the promised help. I can see it in two priests; namely, Father Andrasz and Father Sopocko.** During the retreat before my perpetual vows,[44] I was set completely at peace for the first time [by Father Andrasz], and afterwards I was led in the same direction by Father Sopocko. This was the fulfillment of the Lord's promise.

144   Later Jesus … ordered me to reveal my soul. At first I did so with a bit of hesitation, but a severe reprimand from Jesus brought about a deep humility within my soul. **Under his [confessor's] direction, my soul made quick progress in the love of God,** and many wishes of the Lord were carried out externally. Many a time have I been astounded at his courage and his profound humility.

145   Oh, how wretched my soul is for having wasted so many graces! I was running away from God, and He pursued me with His graces. I most often experienced God's graces when I least expected them. **From the moment He gave me a spiritual director, I have been more faithful to grace.** Thanks to the director and his watchfulness over my soul, I have learned what guidance means and how Jesus looks at it. Jesus warned me of the least fault and stressed that He Himself judges the matter that I present to my confessor; and [He told me]

that... "any transgressions against the confessor touch Me myself."

When **under his direction my soul began to experience deep recollection and peace,** I often heard these words in my soul: "Strengthen yourself for combat — repeated over and over at various times.

+ Jesus often makes known to me what He does not like in my soul, and He has more than once rebuked me for what seemed to be trifles, but which were, in fact, things of great importance. He has warned me and tried me like a Master. For many years, He Himself educated me, until the moment when He gave me a spiritual director. Previously, He Himself had made clear to me what I did not understand; but now, **He tells me to ask my confessor about everything** and often says, "**I will answer you through his mouth. Be at peace.**" It has never happened to me that I have received an answer which was contrary to what the Lord wanted of me, when I presented it to the spiritual director **It sometimes happens that Jesus first asks certain things of me,** about which no one knows anything, and then, when I kneel at the confessional, **my confessor gives me the same order** — however, this is infrequent.

215   "My daughter, be at peace; I am taking all these matters upon Myself. I will arrange all things with your superiors and with the **confessor. Speak to Father Andrasz with the same simplicity and confidence with which you speak to Me.**

263   +The week for confession came and, to my great joy, I saw the priest I had known before coming to Vilnius. [That is to say,] I had known him by seeing him in a vision. At that moment, I heard these words in my soul: **"This is My faithful servant; he will help you to fulfill My will here on earth."** Yet, I did not open myself to him as the Lord

wished. And for some time I struggled against grace. During each confession, God's grace penetrated me in a very special way, yet I did not reveal my soul before him, and I had the intention of not going to confession to that priest. After this decision, a terrible anxiety entered my soul. God reproached me severely. When I did lay bare my soul completely to this priest, Jesus poured an ocean of graces into it. Now I understand what it means to be faithful to a particular grace. That one grace draws down a whole series of others.

293   …In my interior life I never reason; I do not analyze the ways in which God's Spirit leads me. It is enough for me to know that I am loved and that I love. Pure love enables me to know God and understand many mysteries. **My confessor is an oracle [a prophet] for me. His word is sacred to me** — I am speaking about the spiritual director [Father Sopocko].

330   +Once, the confessor told me to pray for his intention, and I began a novena to the Mother of God. This novena consisted in the prayer, "Hail, Holy Queen," recited nine times. Toward the end of the novena I saw the Mother of God with the Infant Jesus in Her arms, and **I also saw my confessor kneeling at Her feet and talking with Her.** I did not understand what he was saying to Her, because I was busy talking with the Infant Jesus, who came down from His Mother's arms and approached me. I could not stop wondering at His beauty. I heard a few of the words that the Mother of God spoke to him [i.e., **my confessor**] but not everything. The words were: "I am not only the Queen of Heaven, but also the Mother of Mercy and your Mother." And at that moment **She stretched out her right hand, in which She was clasping her mantle, and She covered the priest with it.** At that moment, the vision vanished.

422   **Seeing Father Sopocko's sacrifice and efforts for this work, I admired his patience and humility.** This all

cost a great deal, not only in terms of toil and various troubles, but also of money; and Father Sopocko was taking care of all the expenses. I can see that Divine Providence had prepared him to carry out this work of mercy before I had asked God for this. Oh, how strange are Your ways, O God! And how happy are the souls that follow the call of divine grace!

436   June 29, 1935. When **I talked to my spiritual director** [Father Sopocko] about various things that the Lord was asking of me, I thought he would tell me that I was incapable of accomplishing all those things, and that the Lord Jesus did not use miserable souls like me for the works He wanted done. But I heard words [to the effect] that it was just such souls that God chooses most frequently to carry out His plans. **This priest is surely guided by the Spirit of God; he has penetrated the secrets of my soul,** the deepest secrets which were between me and God, about which I had not yet spoken to him, because I had not understood them myself, and the Lord had not clearly ordered me to tell him....

466   Time of Confession.

My confessor [Father Sopocko] asked me if at that moment Jesus was there and if I could see Him. "Yes, He is here, and I can see Him." He then told me to ask Jesus about certain persons. Jesus did not answer me, but looked at him. However, after the confession, when I was reciting my penance, Jesus spoke these words to me: "Go and console him on my behalf." Not understanding the meaning of these words, Immediately repeated to him what Jesus had told me to do.

494   When I was about to go to the parlor to see Father Andrasz, I felt frightened because the secret is binding only in the confessional. This was a groundless fear. One

word from Mother Superior set me at ease about it. Meanwhile, when I entered the chapel, I heard these words in my soul: "**I want you to be open and simple as a child with My representative just as you are with Me;** otherwise I will leave you and will not commune with you."

659   **During Holy Mass, offered by Father Andrasz, I saw the little Infant Jesus,** who told me that I was to depend on him for everything; "no action undertaken on your own, even though you put much effort into it, pleases Me. I understood this [need of] dependence.

675   + August 7, 1936.
When I received the article about Divine Mercy with the image [on the cover], God's presence filled me in an extraordinary way. When I steeped myself in a prayer of thanksgiving, **I suddenly saw the Lord Jesus in a great brightness, just as He is painted, and at His feet I saw Father Andrasz and Father Sopocko.** Both were holding pens in their hands, and **flashes of light and fire, like lightning, were coming from the tips of their pens** and striking a great crowd of people who were hurrying I know not where. Whoever was touched by the ray of light immediately turned his back on the crowd and held out his hands to Jesus. Some returned with great joy, others with great pain and compunction. Jesus was looking at both priests with great kindness. After a while, I was left alone with Jesus, and I said, "Jesus, take me now, for Your will has already been accomplished." And Jesus answered, "My will has not yet been completely accomplished in you; you will still suffer much, but I am with you; do not fear".

676   **I have been talking much with the Lord about Father Andrasz and also about Father Sopocko.** I know that whatever I ask of the Lord He will not refuse me, and He will give them that for which I ask. **I sensed and I know**

how greatly Jesus loves them. I am not writing about this in detail, but I know this, and it makes me very happy.

677   August 15, 1936.
During a Mass celebrated by Father Andrasz, a moment before the Elevation, God's presence pervaded my soul, which was drawn to the altar. Then I saw the Mother of God with the Infant Jesus. The Infant Jesus was holding onto the hand of Our Lady. A moment later, the Infant Jesus ran with joy to the center of the altar, and the Mother of God said to me, "See with what assurance I entrust Jesus into his hands. In the same way, you are to entrust your soul and be like a child to him.

712   **+I saw Father Andrasz today, kneeling and engulfed in prayer, and suddenly Jesus stood by him and, holding out both hands over his head. He said to me: — "He will lead you through; do not fear."**

749   Conversation with Father Andrasz, at the end of the retreat. I was greatly surprised by one thing that I noticed during each conversation in the course of which I had asked advice and direction of Father Andrasz, and it is this: **I noticed that Father Andrasz answered all my questions about things which the Lord has asked of me so clearly and with such assurance that it was as though he were experiencing it all himself.** O my Jesus, if only there were more spiritual directors of this kind, souls under such guidance would very quickly reach the summits of sanctity and would not waste such great graces! I give unceasing thanks to God for so great a grace; namely, that in His great goodness He has deigned to place these pillars of light along the path of my spiritual life. They light my way so that I do not go astray or become delayed in my journey toward close union with the Lord. I have a

great love for the Church, which educates souls and leads them to God.

817   December 13, [1936]. Confession before Jesus.
When I reflected that I had not been to confession for more than three weeks, I wept seeing the sinfulness of my soul and certain difficulties. I had not gone to confession because the circumstances made it impossible. On the day of confessions, I had been confined to bed. The following week, confessions were in the afternoon, and I had left for the hospital that morning. This afternoon, Father Andrasz came into my room and sat down to hear my confession. Beforehand, we did not exchange a single word. I was delighted because I was extremely anxious to go to confession. As usual, I unveiled my whole soul. **Father gave a reply to each little detail.** I felt unusually happy to be able to say everything as I did. For penance, he gave me the Litany of the Holy Name of Jesus. When I wanted to tell him of the difficulty I have in saying this litany, **he rose and began to give me absolution. Suddenly his figure became diffused with a great light, and I saw that it was not Father A., but Jesus.** His garments were bright as snow, and He disappeared immediately. At first, I was a little uneasy, but after a while a kind of peace entered my soul; and I took note of the fact that Jesus heard the confession in the same way that confessors do; and yet something was wondrously transpiring in my heart during this confession; I couldn't at first understand what it signified.

879   I saw Father Andrasz as he was saying Holy Mass today. Before the Elevation, I saw the Infant Jesus with His hands spread out, and He was very joyous; then, after a moment, I saw nothing more. I was in my room and I continued making my thanksgiving. But later on, I thought to myself, **"Why was the Infant Jesus so merry?** After all, He is not always so merry when I see Him." Then I heard these

words interiorly: "**Because I am very much at home in his heart.**" And I was not at all surprised at this, because I know he loves Jesus very much.

967   + When I set to work at underlining the Lord's words and thus was going through everything in sequence, I reached the page where I had marked down **Father Andrasz's** advice and directions. I did not know what to do, to underline or not to underline, and then I heard these words in my soul: "**Underline, because these words are Mine; I have borrowed the lips of the friend of My heart in order to speak to you and reassure you.** You are to observe these directions until your death. It would not please Me at all if you were to disobey these directions. Know that it is I who have placed him between Myself and your soul. I am doing this to set you at peace and so that you may not err."

968   "Since I have placed you in this priest's special care, you are thus exempted from giving a detailed account to your superiors concerning My relationship with you. In all other matters, be as a child with your superiors, but whatever I do in the depths of your soul is to be told, with all frankness, only to the priests."

And I have noticed that, from the time God gave me a spiritual director, He has not required me to report everything to the superiors, as was the case before, but only that which concerns external matters; apart from this, only the director knows my soul. **To have a spiritual director is a special grace of God.** Oh, how few have received it! The soul remains in constant peace amidst the greatest difficulties. Every day after Holy Communion, I thank the Lord Jesus for this grace, and every day I ask the Holy Spirit to enlighten him. I have truly experienced in my soul what power the director's words have. Blessed be God's mercy for this grace!

1012   + March 8, 1937. Today, as **I was praying for the intention of Father Andrasz, I suddenly understood how
intimately this soul communed with God and how
pleasing he was to the Lord.** It gave me immense joy,
because I desire intensely that all souls be united with God
as closely as possible.

1238   August 12. On passing through Cracow, **Reverend Father
Sopocko** paid me a short visit today. I had wanted to see
him, and God fulfilled my desire. **This priest is a great
soul, entirely filled with God.** My joy was very great, and
I thanked God for this great grace, because it was for the
greater glory of God that I wanted to see him.

1256   [August] 30. **Reverend Father Sopocko** left this morning.
When I was steeped in a prayer of thanksgiving for the
great grace that I had received from God; namely, that of
seeing Father, I became united in a special way with the
Lord who said to me, "**He is a priest after My own Heart;
his efforts are pleasing to Me.** You see, My daughter, that
My will must be done and that which I had promised you,
I shall do. Through him I spread comfort to suffering and
careworn souls. Through him it pleased Me to proclaim the
worship of My mercy. **And through this work of mercy
more souls will come close to Me than otherwise would
have, even if he had kept giving absolution day and
night for the rest of his life, because by so doing, he
would have labored only for as long as he lived;
whereas, thanks to this work of mercy, he will be
laboring till the end of the world.**

1346   **During Holy Mass, which was celebrated by Father
Andrasz, I saw the Infant Jesus** who, with hands
outstretched toward us, was sitting in the chalice being
used at Holy Mass. After gazing at me penetratingly, He
spoke these words: "As you see Me in this chalice, so I
dwell in your heart."

1388   + During one time of prayer, I learned how pleasing to God was the soul of **Father Andrasz. He is a true child of God. It is rare that divine sonship shines forth so clearly in a soul, and this because he has a special devotion to the Mother of God.**

1390   I see **Father Sopocko**, how his mind is busily occupied and working in God's cause in order to present the wishes of God to the officials of the Church. As a result of his efforts, a new light will shine in the Church of God for the consolation of souls. Although for the present his soul is filled with bitterness, as though that were to be the reward for his efforts in the cause of the Lord, this will not however be the case. I see his joy, which nothing will diminish. God will grant him some of this joy already here on earth. **I have never before come upon such great faithfulness to God as distinguishes this soul.**

1401   Yesterday I received a letter from **Father Sopocko**. I learned that God's work is progressing, however slowly. I am very happy about this, and I have redoubled my prayers for this entire work. I have come to learn that, for the present, so far as my participation in the work is concerned, the Lord is asking for prayer and sacrifice. Action on my part could indeed thwart God's plans, as Father Sopocko wrote in yesterday's letter. O my Jesus, grant me the grace to be an obedient instrument in Your hands. **I have learned from this letter how great is the light which God grants to this priest.** This confirms me in the conviction that God will carry out this work through him despite the mounting obstacles. I know well that the greater and the more beautiful the work is, the more terrible will be the storms that rage against it.

1408   I was present at Holy Mass celebrated by **Father Sopocko.** During the Mass, I saw the Infant Jesus who, touching the priest's forehead with His finger, said to me, **"His thought is closely united to Mine, so be at peace about what concerns My work.** I will not let him make a mistake, and you should do nothing without his permission." This filled my soul with great peace as regards everything that has to do with this work.

1472   January 8. During Holy Mass, I had a moment of knowledge concerning **Father S., that great glory is being given to God through our mutual efforts.** And even though we are far from each other, we are often together, because we are united by a common goal.

1544   "Do not change your particular examen which I have given you through Father Andrasz; namely, that you unite yourself with Me continually. That is what I am clearly asking of you today. **Be a child toward My representatives, because I borrow their lips to speak to you, so that you will have no doubts about anything."**

1547   Today I saw the efforts of this **priest** [Father Sopocko] concerning the affairs of God. **His heart is beginning to taste that which filled God's Heart during His earthly life. In recompense for his efforts — ingratitude...** But he is very zealous for the glory of God...

Appendix II

THE CHURCH AND THE DIVINE MERCY
DEVOTION

November 28, 1958 — Sister Faustina's written prophecy about the apparent destruction of the devotion to The Divine Mercy begins to be fulfilled in the form of a decree of condemnation from the Holy See, severely banning the Divine Mercy devotion.

March 6, 1959 — The severe ban is mitigated by Pope John XXIII and replaced by a "Notification" prohibiting "the spreading of images and writings that promote the devotion of The Divine Mercy *in the forms proposed by the same Sister Faustina.*"

October 21, 1965 — Archbishop Karol Wojtyla begins the Informative Process relating to the life and virtues of Sister Faustina. From this moment, Sister Faustina is worthy of the title "Servant of God."

June 26, 1967 — Archbishop Wojtyla becomes Karol Cardinal Wojtyla.

September 20, 1967 — Archbishop Karol Cardinal Wojtyla officially closes the first informative stage in the process for the beatification of the Servant of God Sister Faustina Kowalska.

The outcome of the Process of Information shows that the action in Rome with regard to Sister Faustina was taken (at the least) on insufficient evidence. (Official communications between Rome and the Church in Poland during those post-war years, especially with regard to religious matters, were very difficult. Relevant, authentic documents could not be made available to the investigating authorities who were being pressed to make a judgment on the matter presented to them.)

January 31, 1968 — By a Decree of the Sacred Congregation for the Causes of Saints, the Process of Beatification of the Servant of God Sister Faustina H. Kowalska is formally inaugurated.

June 30, 1978 — The Sacred Congregation issues a new "Notification" declaring the prohibitions of 1959 no longer binding.

October 16, 1978 — Karol Cardinal Wojtyla becomes Pope John Paul II.

July 12, 1979 — The Congregation of Marians receive a letter clarifying the Notification of 1978. It states:
"… there no longer exists, on the part of this Sacred Congregation, any impediment to the spreading of the devotion to The Divine Mercy in the authentic forms proposed by the Religious sister mentioned above [the Servant of God, Sister Faustina Kowalska].

November 30, 1980 — Pope John Paul II publishes his encyclical letter, *Rich in Mercy.*

April 18, 1984 — The Process for the verification of an alleged cure through the intercession of Sister Faustina is begun in the Metropolitan Archdiocese of Cracow, Poland.

November 4, 1986 — On the Feast of St. Charles, nameday for Karol Wojtyla (Pope John Paul II), the process concerning the alleged cure is completed in Cracow, and Cardinal Francis Macharski sends the official documents to Rome,

November 10, 1986 — The documents are received in Rome by the Postulator, Father Antoni Mruk, S.J.

January 22, 1987 — Fr. Mruk presents the documents to the Sacred Congregation for the Causes of Saints.

February 12, 1987 — The Sacred Congregation issues a decree stating that the documents have been received and officially opened.

February 10, 1989 — Doctor Mario Meschini, a well-known medical doctor and brother of a doctor on the medical commission of the Sacred Congregation for the Causes of Saints, writes a private, professional opinion concerning the alleged cure. He states that the cure was very rapid, complete, and lasting, and that it would most likely be recognized by the Sacred Congregation as miraculous in nature.

February 12, 1991 — All the documents concerning the heroic virtue of Sister Faustina are completed and sent to the Sacred Congregation.

April 10, 1991 — Pope John Paul II, at his general audience spoke about Sister Faustina, showing his great respect for her, relating her to his encyclical, *Rich in Mercy*, and emphasizing her role in bringing the message of mercy to the world.

March 7, 1992 — Pope John Paul II signs the Decree of Heroicity, by which the Church acknowledges that Sister Faustina practiced all the Christian virtues to an heroic degree. Thus, she may now be called "Venerable."

April 18, 1993 — The Venerable Servant of God, Sister Maria Faustina Kowalska, is beatified by Pope John Paul II in Rome on the first Sunday after Easter, which is celebrated by many around the world as Divine Mercy Sunday.

April 30, 2000 — Blessed Maria Faustina Kowalska is canonized by Pope John Paul II in Rome on Divine Mercy Sunday as the first saint of the Great Jubilee Year of the Incarnation. John Paul II also announces in his homily that "the Second Sunday of Easter from now on throughout the Church will be called 'Divine Mercy Sunday.'"

April 22, 2001 — The Church celebrates Divine Mercy Sunday as a universal feast for the first time.

Appendix III

THE EASTER MESSAGE OF
THE MERCIFUL CHRIST

Pope John Paul II

General Audience 10 April 1991

(**L'OSSERVATORE ROMANO**, English edition, 15 April 1991, p. 11.)

1. "In the name of Jesus Christ crucified and risen, in the spirit of his messianic mission, enduring in the history of humanity, we raise our voices and pray that the love which is in the Father may once again *be revealed at this stage of history* and that, through the work of the Son and Holy Spirit, it may be shown to be present in our modern world and to be more powerful than evil: more powerful than sin and death.

"We pray for this through the intercession of her who does not cease to proclaim 'mercy … from generation to generation', and also through the intercession of those for whom there have been completely fulfilled the words of the Sermon on the Mount: "Blessed are the merciful, for they shall obtain mercy' " (*Dives in Misericordia*, 15).

2. Our Lady of Jasna Gora! *The words of the encyclical on divine mercy* (*Dives in Misericordia*) are particularly close to us. They recall the figure of the Servant of God, Sister Faustina Kowalska. This simple woman religious particularly brought *the Easter message of the merciful Christ* closer to Poland and the whole world.

This happened before the Second World War and all its cruelty. In the face of all the organized contempt for the human person, the message of Christ who was tormented and rose again became for many people in Poland and beyond its borders, and even on other continents, a *source of the hope and strength necessary for survival.*

3. And Today? Is it perhaps not necessary also "in the contemporary world" in our homeland, in society, among the people who have entered into a new phase of our history, *for love to reveal that it is stronger than hatred and selfishness?* Is it perhaps not necessary to translate into the language of today's generations the words of the Gospel, "blessed are the merciful, for they shall obtain mercy" (Mt 5:7)?

O Mother, who announces divine mercy "from generation to generation" (Lk 1:50), help our generation to rise from the moral crisis. May Christ's new commandment, "love one another" (Jn 13:34) be established ever more fully among us.

Commentary

Pope John Paul II's brief reflection is significant in several ways:

† It identifies the message of mercy as the Easter message of the merciful Christ, thus emphasizing the significance of the Feast of Mercy as the octave celebration of Easter Sunday (#2).

† It links Mary's role in announcing mercy "from generation to generation" with Sister Faustina's role in bringing the message of mercy "closer to Poland and the whole world' (#1, par 2; & #2, par 1).

† It implies that, just as we pray for mercy through the intercession of Mary, "who does not cease to proclaim mercy," so

we should also pray through the intercession of Sister Faustina, who is an example of those who have received the promise of the beatitude, "Blessed are the merciful, for they shall obtain mercy" (#1, par 2; & #2, par 1).

† It underscores the necessity for us to proclaim and live out the message of mercy in order to heal the moral problems of our contemporary world (#3).